Nature Photography

Nature Photography

LOCATION & STUDIO WORKSHOP

TEXT AND PHOTOGRAPHS BY

Arnold Wilson

DESIGNED BY
GRANT BRADFORD

FOUNTAIN PRESS

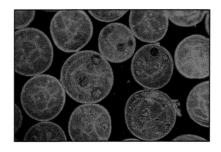

Published by
Fountain Press
Newpro UK Limited
Old Sawmills Road
Faringdon
Oxfordshire
England SN7 7DS

© Fountain Press, Newpro UK Ltd
2001

Original Images
© Arnold Wilson

Text & Photographs
ARNOLD WILSON

Design & Layout
GRANT BRADFORD

Illustrations
Kuo Kang Chen

Origination
New Century Colour
Hong Kong

Printing & Binding
Die Keure n.v.
Belgium

ISBN 0 86343 348 0

FOREWORD

This book has been written with two groups of people in mind: the serious amateur or semi-professional photographer who has mastered the basics of photography and is developing an interest in natural history and the person who is primarily a naturalist and would like to take better quality photographs of plants and animals in the field.

An introduction, which discusses the resourcefulness and practical approach of the nature photographer, is followed by two short chapters on cameras, lenses and accessories which are of particular interest to the nature photographer, ending with an introduction to close-up and microscopy techniques. Another early chapter considers composition and the general organisation of the image, which is not only very important but fundamental to the whole concept of the book.

The main body of the book concentrates on individual assignments or projects grouped under chapter headings such as 'Woodlands', 'Cliffs and the Seashore' and 'Rivers, Streams and Ponds'. My approach is a very practical one with each assignment consisting of a brief introduction to the organism; mainly basic ecology plus any features which are unusual and of particular interest. This is followed by the middle section where I describe in detail how each particular assignment was done, including information about equipment, time of day, month of the year and any problems which may have arisen. I have tried, wherever possible, to capture some of the action associated with the animals, such as insects and birds flying, frogs leaping, newts swimming and foxes bolting. In the plant kingdom, movement is exemplified by the ingenious mechanisms which have evolved for the dispersal of seeds, spores and pollen. In the section on pond life I have introduced some basic photomicrography to illustrate how exciting images of the micro-world are well within the grasp of any enthusiastic photographer.

The final section of each assignment consists of one (or occasionally two) selected photograph, printed large and discussed critically for its content, composition, lighting etc., highlighting the deficiencies and weaknesses as well as the more obvious positive qualities.

By its very nature, much of the work included in this book had to be done in Britain, but I have also photographed in Brittany, Slovenia (former Yugoslavia), southern Spain, northern Italy, Germany, Iceland and Singapore, with images from these areas included where appropriate.

The manufacturers of cameras, accessories and other equipment mentioned in the book, together with conservation organisations and licensing authorities are all listed at the end of the book.

Arnold Wilson

Leeds 2001

CONTENTS

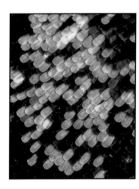

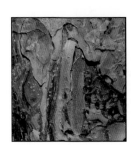

CHAPTER ONE

Introduction

In an ideal world light levels would always be just right, winds non-existent, and animals and birds would continue feeding as we approached to within a few metres to take our photographs. Very, very occasionally the 'ideal world' conditions come simultaneously and we capture an impressive image, but for most of the time it is a constant struggle calling for patience and ingenuity.

Nature photographers are a very inventive breed and though more gadgets and equipment are becoming available commercially, anyone with a few basic tools and a little nous can develop and build useful gadgets or even more sophisticated equipment, to help capture those elusive once-in-a-lifetime shots. I enjoy designing and making things and over the years have put this to good use in my nature photography. In the garage is a large collection of nuts, bolts, screws, pieces of timber and hardboard, plus off-cuts of aluminium and mild steel, all 'left-overs' from household and car maintenance tasks saved on the premise that 'they might come in useful one day'.

To most animals in the wild, man is a dangerous predator best avoided, and therefore getting sufficiently close to obtain a decent-sized image calls for a degree of resourcefulness, occasionally aided by modern technology. The usual method is to work from a hide (or blind, as it is known in the States) and at the turn of the century wildlife photographers Richard and Cherry Kearton used the mounted skin of a cow to get close to the birds. But it soon became clear that posing as another animal was not really necessary and the first hide, resembling a camper's toilet for midgets, was soon on the market. It came complete with a substantial frame, guy-ropes and pegs, and though still available today in this form, it has to a large extent been superseded by lightweight collapsible units which will fit into a pocket in a rucksack.

If the animal or bird returns frequently to the feeding site, a hide can sometimes be built nearby from local materials, such as brushwood and branches (in woodland) or rocks and pebbles (on the seashore). When I was photographing swallows in a derelict barn, I built a hide across one corner from lengths of old timber and corrugated-steel sheeting lying around on the floor. Another photographer uses an old canoe as a hide, attaching appropriate vegetation to it before lying prone and slowly paddling out towards the water birds.

Left: Modern hides, like this one from Wildlife Watching Supplies, are light, compact and very easy to erect. They are well camouflaged to fit in with a variety of habitats.

Right: A well-camouflaged bag hide with a scrim-net opening window and a large Velcro-adjustable lens opening. Produced by Wildlife Watching Supplies.

An elephant hawkmoth, Deilephila elpenor, photographed in the home-made flight tunnel using the solenoid release unit described on page 11. This photograph was overall winner in the Wildlife Photographer of the Year competition.

The original electro-mechanical release unit, designed and built several years ago, was used to produce some quite successful images. When the solenoid circuit is momentarily closed, the soft iron core is magnetically attracted into the solenoid, releasing a spring-loaded arm which depresses the cable release, firing the camera and flash units.

This shot was taken from a hide in the corner of the barn, built from lengths of old timber and pieces of corrugated-steel sheeting lying about on the floor.
The camera and flash units were triggered using a hand-held bell-push switch at the end of a length of twin electrical flex linked to the camera autowinder via a 2.5mm jack plug.

Several companies now produce excellent lightweight camouflage materials to suit different types of environment and seasons of the year. They are well ventilated and can be pulled over the photographer and his camera providing excellent cover. All these man-made hides seem to work surprisingly well but as the visual acuity of many birds is often as much as six times greater than ours, I do sometimes wonder if they are really deceived by our elaborate but often clumsy attempts to conceal ourselves.

Cameras can be left in position and triggered remotely by the photographer comfortably ensconced many metres away. Laurie Campbell, the well-known Scottish wildlife photographer, has a purpose-made but quite nondescript-looking wooden box with a camera inside, which he leaves among the pebbles on the seashore, triggering the camera and autowind remotely from the comfort of his parked camper van. This allows him to fire off a whole roll of film without ever approaching the camera.

Many years ago I bought a reel (15 metres, 50 ft) of household twin electrical flex, fixed a 2.5mm plug to one end to link it to the camera's autowinder, and a domestic bell-push switch to the other end. This has proved to be one of my most successful and frequently used accessories, instrumental in producing many 'swallow-in-flight' and woodland-bird photographs. Radio remote triggers are now available at a reasonable price (see Appendix) which can fire the camera and flash units from up to 100 metres away. The infrared light beam switch is another useful accessory which when set up, for example, across the entrance to a badger sett, will trigger the camera and flash units when the badger leaves the sett.

I am particularly interested in photographing insects in flight, prompting me, several years ago, to design a simple flight tunnel and a white light beam triggering device. The latter was built using bits and pieces from my store of 'useful things', plus a photographic lens and some electronic components purchased locally. As an Olympus OM autowinder was not available at the time, I designed and built an electro-mechanical release unit which triggered the camera and flash units via a standard cable release.

Light is essential to produce a photographic image and many nature photographers prefer to carry 'daylight' around with them rather than relying on the unpredictable weather in the northern hemisphere. Instead of using just one flash unit attached to the camera body, I usually link several together well away from the camera, to boost the light output or shorten the flash duration. Three linked Metz 45s are often used; two as a main light and the third as a fill-in, supported on either an extendable lightweight aluminium pole bought from a local angling shop, or attached to a tree trunk via a small G-clamp/screwed spike accessory. Three Olympus T32s are used in the flight tunnel producing exposures as short as 1/15,000 sec, sufficient to 'freeze' the 150 wing-beats per second of a bumblebee in free flight.

A short-range (up to 50 metres) Jama radio remote control unit consisting of a hand-held transmitter which sends a signal to the receiver which in turn triggers the camera and flash units via the autowinder. It was used at a distance of around 30 metres to photograph a fox at night. (see page 128 for details.)

A car can often function as a hide, with the camera supported on a beanbag and well camouflaged. Some camera supports clip over the car window or frame but are often not quite as stable as the trusty old beanbag.

Other useful home-made gadgets include a ground spike with a ball-and-socket head attached, for supporting a camera or flash unit down at ground level; white, silver or gold cardboard cake-bases as small reflectors in close-up work; and a beanbag, made up in canvas or linen (23 x 20cm, 9 x 8in), filled with dried peas and used as a camera support. A tripod and camera can be stabilised on a windy day by suspending a large stone or brick (or even your camera bag) from the centre post, when it will also hold the tripod down and lower its centre of gravity.

'Make-it-yourself' gadgetry is not just the preserve of the stills photographer; witness the wildlife films produced by the BBC Natural History Unit in Bristol. Films which describe how the various series were made, illustrate the incredible inventiveness of the film makers with their camera-carrying, floating model of a hippopotamus head; radio-controlled model aeroplanes complete with camera; and the made-to-measure camera-carrying harness snugly fitted to a goose's body.

These very useful gadgets and accessories can certainly make wildlife photography easier, but without detailed knowledge of the animal or plant's ecology, life cycle and, most importantly, its location, they will remain unused.

A nature photographer is a combination of photographer, naturalist and handyman; the first two are essential, the latter is an added bonus, but a very valuable one.

Prize winning shot of bumblebee in free flight using make-it-yourself gadgetry. The flight tunnel (still in use) and the interrupted light beam trigger switch (now replaced by a commercial unit) were both designed and built in the garage. Exposure: multiple flash, f16, Kodak Elite 100.

Fox in early evening sunshine After regular feeding over a six-month period the fox ocassionally paid us a daylight visit. Here it waits patiently for its evening meal. Exposure 1/15 sec, f11, 500mm lens, Fuji Sensia 100.

CHAPTER TWO

Cameras & Lenses

When it comes to choosing a suitable type of camera for nature or wildlife photography, it is really a one-horse race with the 35mm single lens reflex (SLR) camera winning hands down. It is lightish, robust, has a bright accurate viewing system, through the lens (TTL) metering, an excellent range of shutter speeds and the ability to accept an assortment of lenses from 'fish eyes' to long telephotos.

Other types of camera which are not suitable for various reasons include the compact and APS – parallax problems and fixed lens; studio – much too bulky and slow; twin-lens reflex – parallax problems and very few interchangeable lenses; Polaroid – expensive film and not versatile; digital – too expensive at present, but likely to be the camera of the future.

If your SLR camera is to be versatile and able to tackle all types of nature photography, it should be a 'systems camera', that is one for which there is a wide range of lenses and accessories available from the manufacturer. Names which spring to mind are Nikon (used by most professionals in all branches of photography), Canon, Minolta, Pentax, and Olympus, although in their OM range, Olympus now only produce the manual focus OM-4Ti and OM-3Ti (plus their fixed lens IS series) with lenses and accessories difficult to obtain and very expensive. Independent lens manufacturers rarely include Olympus fittings.

LARGER FORMAT SLR CAMERAS

While most wildlife photographers prefer the 35mm format for reasons of weight, bulk and price, the larger medium formats (4.5 x 6cm, 6 x 6cm, and 6 x 7cm) are readily available from Mamiya, Bronica, Pentax and Hasselblad. Photographers are attracted to them because they require less enlargement and produce better image quality and lower granularity, although in practice the differences are less than you might expect.

Two shots of spring snowdrops taken from the same position.

Left: With the 28mm wide-angle lens fully open (f 3.5) and focused on the nearest flowers.

Right: With the lens stopped down to f 16 and focused slightly further back to obtain the maximum benefit from the greatly increased depth of field, clearly visible in the viewfinder using the preview button or lever.

Tulip image showing almost perfect bilateral symmetry, taken using the ever popular 50mm macro lens. This lens will focus from infinity down to half life-size without any loss of resolving power. Exposure: 1/60 sec, f16, Kodak Elite 100.

A pair of marine fanworms (Sabella) with the expanded fan or feather-like radioles projecting from the top of the sand and mucous tube. The radioles sway around in the water filter feeding small food particles. When disturbed, the feathery crown is reflexly withdrawn into the tube. Exposure: flash, f16, 120mm macro lens, Pentax 645N, Fuji Velvia ISO 50.

Black-headed gull, Larus ridibundus, 'frozen' in flight. I set the camera on 1/1000 second shutter priority, allowing the camera's meter to select the appropriate aperture which was f 8 using Kodak Elite 200 film.

Medium format SLR cameras cost more than double the price and are much bulkier and heavier than similar quality 35mm SLR cameras. The lenses are very heavy due to the weight of glass in them and cost at least three times more than their 35mm equivalents. The total weight of an outfit containing a couple of bodies and a range of lenses can become a very significant consideration when it has to be carried miles over rough terrain.

Yet despite these disadvantages, the Bronica ETRSi, the Mamiya 645E and AF and the Pentax 645N are very popular with nature photographers who hope that the larger size will give their images that extra bite and quality.

USEFUL FEATURES

A 35 mm SLR camera to be used for wide-ranging nature photography should embody most of the following features.

A bright pentaprism viewing system allows the camera to be used at eye level with the image the right way round. All 35mm SLRs have a built-in pentaprism but it is usually an extra on most medium format SLRs (Pentax 645 and Contax 645 excepted).

Due to the instant return mirror, which is now standard on all 35mm SLRs, the viewed image is continuous except for the 1/25

second or so when the mirror is up to allow the exposure to be made. When long exposures are required, it is very useful to be able to lock up the mirror to help prevent mirror-induced vibrations affecting the sharpness of the image. Unfortunately this very useful feature is not available on most of today's cameras, although on some the mirror locks up when the delayed action mechanism is used, which is fine as long as the subject remains still during the 10 seconds or so count-down.

The standard matte focusing screen with its microprism and rangefinder centre will cover most requirements, but if the screen is interchangeable it is worth investing in an all-matte screen for long telephoto work and a cross-hairs clear centre screen if you intend to do any photomicrography. I use a Beattie screen (American import) which brightens up the image by up to 2 stops; very useful when using a long 'slowish' telephoto lens in poor light.

A 'preview' button or lever allows the lens to be stopped down to the set aperture so that the depth of field can be seen and assessed. Unfortunately most modern 35 mm SLRs have lost this facility, which is a great pity.

Wood anemones, Anemone nemorosa, in spring.

Left: Taken with a standard 50 mm lens does not show the characteristics of the background. Exposure: 1/2 sec, f 16. Fuji Velvia.

Right: Using a close-focusing 24 mm wide-angle lens, the anemones are still sufficiently large in the frame but the background indicates that they are part of a carpet of flowers in a woodland clearing. Exposure: 1/4 sec, f 16. Fuji Velvia.

Nowadays the range of shutter speeds is quite incredible, often going from a heady 1/8,000 second (or 1/12,000 second in the latest Minolta 9xi) to 30 seconds, which to me looks like another example of technology for technology's sake. At the 'short' end I occasionally use the 1/1,000-second speed while 4 seconds is about the longest exposure I can recall using. For longish exposures the shutter should be triggered without touching the camera, by using a cable release (a feature on current cameras and well worth having) or a plug-in electrical cable release and switch (usually available as an accessory).

EXPOSURE METERS

Although separate hand-held exposure meters are often preferred by professional photographers (most medium format SLRs have no built-in metering as standard), all modern 35 mm SLR cameras have an exposure system as an integral part of the camera's design. In an effort to produce 'better' exposed negatives and transparencies, more and more sophisticated systems have been developed, including the original centre-weighted metering with approximately 60 per cent of the final reading taken from the central area, where it is assumed that the main subject lies. Some cameras also have spot metering in which a tiny central spot, representing about 2 per cent of the total image area, is selected for exposure assessment, or multi-spot metering where the camera microprocessor averages out several spot readings. Finally, in multi-zone or multi-segment metering, light values are measured in up to six segments of the image field with the camera computing the readings to produce the 'best' exposure, a system which is very effective in difficult lighting conditions.

All exposure meters are calibrated to produce the 'correct' exposure on the assumption that the subject is reflecting 18 per cent of the light falling on it and rather surprisingly lots of animals, plants and landscapes do. When the subject reflects much less than 18 per cent, in for example the classic case of a black cat in a coal cellar, the meter will indicate a much longer exposure, with the black cat registering grey. Similarly snow, white blossom or bright yellow flowers will be underexposed and appear grey or dull yellow respectively in the final image.

The magnifying power of the telephoto lens. Countryside view using the standard 50mm lens

Taken from the same position with a 250mm lens.

A 500mm lens highlights the farmhouse and its associated buildings.
All exposures: 1/4 sec, f 16. Fuji Velvia.

Silver birch, Betulina pendula, dispersing pollen. Taken indoors using flash units at either side and slightly behind the catkins. A 'straight' meter reading would have 'washed out' the catkins and lightened the black background. I overrode the meter reading, underexposing by $1^1/_3$ stops.

Perspective distortion using wide-angle and telephoto lenses. The camera was moved back and forth so that the group of daffodils was the same size on each photograph.

Left: 24mm wide-angle lens used.

Centre: Standard 50mm lens produces the same perspective as the human eye.

Above: 300mm lens foreshortens the perspective and reduces the depth of field.

All exposures: 1/4 sec, f 22.

Many years ago Kodak marketed a grey card (still available today) which produced 18 per cent reflectance and when it was held in front of the camera to almost fill the field of view, an accurate reading would be obtained, with snow registering white and black cats, black. Medium-red roses, green grass and my grey anorak have similar reflectance levels to the grey card. An experienced photographer will be aware of non-standard reflecting subjects and will have the confidence to take control and adjust the exposure accordingly, using the camera's '+' and '–' exposure compensation button. If this is unavailable, the only alternative is to temporarily change the film speed setting on the camera. For example to underexpose by 2/3 stop, change the setting from say ISO 50 to 80, or from ISO 100 to 160.

All the metering systems discussed so far measure the light reflected from the subject but an alternative method is to measure the light falling on the subject. This is incident light measurement, whose value is not subject to the colours or tones of the subject being photographed.

A translucent hemisphere is slid over the hand-held meter and, with the photographer standing in front of the subject, the meter is pointed in the direction of the sun and a reading taken. Many professionals (particularly landscape and portrait photographers) prefer this method, slow as it is, but most nature photographers are quite happy to use the fast-acting, reflected light exposure system built into their cameras.

EXPOSURE MODES

Most SLR cameras provide a range of exposure modes to satisfy the differing needs of photographers. The 'programme' mode allows no choice of aperture or shutter speed and is of little value to the nature photographer. I am quite happy with only two modes: aperture priority, where I set the aperture while the camera selects the appropriate shutter speed, and fully 'manual', where both the aperture and shutter speed are under my control. For about 90 per cent of my work I use aperture priority as the aperture, and therefore the depth of field, is usually more important than the shutter speed. Shutter priority is useful when photographing, for example, birds in flight or animals on the move, but even with aperture priority you can set a wide aperture and secure the short exposure you require.

Peacock butterfly, Inachis io, flying towards a church window. Actually I frabricated the background and the peacock is flying along a flight tunnel. Exposure: 50mm macro lens, multiple flash, f16, Fuji Velvia ISO 50.

Of the total number of 35 mm SLR cameras available today, just over half are autofocus, which in its latest incarnation can focus faster and more accurately than can be achieved by hand, although in the early years this was not always the case. If I were buying a new camera today I would certainly opt for autofocus, but would select one with a wide manual focus ring for easy handling. (Many of the early models had an almost useless, very thin ring.) Check that the camera has an efficient focus-hold facility as only rarely is the main subject right in the centre of the frame where the autofocus area is located. In 1997 Pentax introduced the first medium format autofocus camera with their updated 645N model, while some two years later Contax followed with their own 645 autofocus camera – Mamiya launched their 645AF autofocus camera in 1999.

LENSES

In recent years lens development has progressed apace, helped by computer-aided design (CAD), the use of low dispersion glasses and the introduction of aspheric lenses (lens surfaces which are not part of a sphere like 'conventional' spheric lenses). Overall resolution and contrast have increased, while lens aberrations such as astigmatism, pin-cushion and barrel distortion and spherical aberration are almost non-existent in the best of today's lenses. Most are still described as 'achromatic' (meaning 'no colour fringe'), where the blue and red rays are brought to a focus at the same point.

In the very best telephoto lenses, chromatic aberration has been virtually eliminated as blue, red and green rays come to the same point of focus. These lenses are described as 'aprochromatic' (APO).

Internal focusing (IF) is becoming quite common with the advantage that the lens length does not change during focusing, thereby maintaining a better balance on the camera, while the non-rotating lens barrel is of great benefit when using a matched flower-shaped lens hood or creative and polarising filters.

Many zoom lenses now have a greater range than ever, with 28–300mm becoming increasingly popular, as lens bodies become progressively shorter and lighter; the latter due to the use of lightweight polycarbonate plastics in place of traditional steel and aluminium alloys. Most lenses are competitively priced, particularly those from manufacturers such as Tamron, Sigma and Tokina.

STANDARD LENS

The standard lens for a 35mm SLR camera has a focal length of 50mm (75mm for the 4.5 x 6cm and 6 x 6cm formats and 90mm for the 6 x 7 cm format), with a maximum aperture of around f1.8. It is referred to as 'standard' because it produces roughly the same perspective as the human eye (but a much narrower angle of view – 40° against 160° using both eyes). The standard lens is a highly corrected optic with at least six elements, focusing down to around 35cm (14 in) making it suitable for subjects ranging from mountain landscapes to close-ups of flowers and large insects. Used in the reverse position it will function as an excellent macro lens producing high quality images of life size and larger. (Macro lenses are discussed in some detail in Chapter 4.)

WARM-UP FILTERS AND THEIR EFFECT

Left: River scene taken in early June without any filters.

Below: River scene using an amber 81C filter. Although the colour cast produced here is artificial, normal sunlight does vary greatly in its 'warmth' or 'coldness' throughout the day, with strong red light as the sun rises and sets, and blue light when the sky is leaden and overcast.

WIDE-ANGLE LENSES

These lenses have shorter focal lengths than the standard lens, ranging from 38mm down to 16mm 'fish eyes', and produce a much wider field of view. This can be an obvious advantage because the image includes much more information, but the perspective is progressively distorted with distant objects appearing much further away than they look to the human eye. The effect can be particularly disappointing when photographing mountains. This assumes the picture being looked at is held some 12 in (30cm) from the eyes. When brought in much closer, the perspective becomes more faithful to the original scene.

I use a wide-angle lens mainly to illustrate flowers or animals in their natural surroundings where the subject can be shown in close-up, against the background of which it is an integral part. Extreme wide-angle lenses produce so much distortion that they are of little use to the nature photographer.

Polarising filters can deepen blue skies, cut out reflections from leaves and petals and from water surfaces, but at the expense of up to 2 stops of light.

Left: Pond with highly reflective surface. Floating duckweed is visible, whereas the underwater pondweed is almost invisible.

Right: The polarising filter has brightened up the greens of the rushes, grasses and floating pondweed, while removing much of the water surface reflection, allowing the underwater pondweed to show up.

TELEPHOTO LENSES

These lenses have operating focal lengths ranging from a modest 90mm to a very substantial 600 or even 1,000mm, with a good spread between. The main and obvious function of a long-focus lens is to magnify the image, with the degree of magnification being proportional to the focal length; for example a 500mm lens will produce an image 10 times larger than the standard 50mm lens can achieve.

Other characteristics are a flattening or foreshortening of the perspective, a greatly reduced depth of field, coupled with the likelihood of producing unsharp images due to camera shake if the camera is hand-held. As a rule of thumb, the shutter speed should be no longer than the reciprocal of the focal length of the lens (image-stabilising lenses excepted), so that hand-holding a 300mm lens would require a camera shutter speed of 1/300 second or shorter. Hence the golden rule of always using a tripod.

The shorter telephoto lenses (e.g. 90–200mm) are useful when photographing individual flowers, butterflies, moths and bees in close-up without having to approach closer than 1–2 metres. An added advantage is that the depth of field becomes progressively shallower as the focal length increases, making it quite easy and very effective to throw the background well out of focus (producing the opposite effect to a wide-angle lens in a similar situation).

The extra-powerful 500 and 600mm lenses are ideal for producing large images of birds and mammals which are difficult to approach, but these long lenses are more difficult to use successfully, requiring very accurate focusing and a firm support. They are also heavy and expensive, with the price rising dramatically as the maximum aperture increases. A top quality Canon AF 400mm f 5.6L lens costs over £1,000 while Canon's 400mm f 2.8 L lens is almost £5,000. However, the latter transmits four times more light than the f 5.6 lens, allowing a 2 stop increase in the aperture or a shortening of the exposure to a quarter of that required by the f 5.6 lens. The viewfinder image is much brighter, making work in poor light that much easier.

A cheaper alternative to the conventional long-focus lens is the catadioptric or 'mirror' lens, which is light and compact but suffers from having a very modest fixed aperture (usually f 8 in a 500mm lens) with no control of the depth of field. A curious, quite off-putting side effect is that out-of-focus highlights on water appear as doughnut-shaped rings.

This portrait of a puffin illustrates the value of using a long telephoto lens to produce a large image at a workable distance. The puffin would not allow me to approach closer than about 6 metres but the telephoto lens came to the rescue. The sideways glance shows the multi-coloured beak to advantage while the out-of-focus background makes the whole bird stand out. Exposure: 1/30 sec, f11, 500mm lens, Fuji Sensia 100.

Zoom lenses have become increasingly popular in recent years with their optical quality about on a par with fixed focal length lenses. The obvious advantage is that you can frame the scene to obtain good subject size and composition without having to walk back and forth. A real bonus is that a 28–300mm zoom lens will replace a bagful of fixed focal length lenses, while on the downside zoom lens apertures tend to be modest, with f 4.5–f 5.6 being quite common. Finally, it is worth noting that the very best APO-type lenses using low dispersion glasses, tend to have a limited zoom ratio of about 4 or less (e.g. Sigma 75–300mm APO or Canon L 70–200mm).

TELECONVERTERS

A teleconverter (or multiplier) is a highly corrected concave lens assembly containing up to half a dozen elements, which fits between the camera lens and the body, magnifying the image produced by the camera lens. They are available in different strengths ranging from x1.4 to x4, and at face value look like a photographer's dream come true. Simply add a x2 converter to your modest 300mm lens and it becomes a mighty 600mm blockbuster! However, there are several drawbacks. Unless the converter is designed by the camera manufacturer for their own lenses, it may not perform well with other makes of lens resulting in a degraded image. Doubling the focal length (using a x2 converter) without increasing the lens diameter will reduce the effective aperture by 2 stops converting a 300mm f 5.6 lens into a very slow 600mm f 11 lens. Some of the teleconverters (mainly x1.4 and x2) produced by mainstream manufacturers are a good investment but avoid the cheaper ones (particularly the older models) made by various independent companies. I have a good quality x1.4 Sigma converter which works well with my Sigma 75–300mm APO lens, and a x2 converter for my Pentax 645 camera, which also produces excellent results.

The fact that a teleconverter does not affect the minimum focusing distance of the main lens was put to good use recently when I was photographing a tropical pitcher plant. At the minimum focusing distance of 0.6 m (2 ft) the pitcher was much too small but adding the converter doubled the image size, resulting in a very satisfactory shot.

LENS HOOD AND FILTERS

A lens hood prevents light not involved in forming the image from entering the camera lens. Light from outside the image area can reduce contrast and produce lens flare as it reflects off the inside of the lens barrel and glass elements.

Basic lens hoods are black, circular and internally ribbed, while more effective ones are rectangular with the same height/length ratio as the negative. The very best are adjustable bellows units, rarely seen on 35mm SLRs but quite common on medium format cameras. Buy the best you can afford and remember to use it!

I only use filters occasionally, as most nature shots do not require artificial enhancement. Another two glass–air surfaces in front of the camera lens could marginally degrade the image, should the filter be marked or slightly greasy. A polarising filter will cut out surface reflections and increase the colour saturation of grass and blue sky, while an amber warm-up filter (81A and 81C) will brighten up a rather cold scene. I also use neutral density filters to reduce the overall light level without changing the colour balance and neutral density graduated filters to darken an overlit sky.

FILM TYPES AND SPEED

All my nature photography is done on slide film and over the years I have used Kodak Ektachrome and Elite, but in recent times I have drifted towards Fujichrome film, partly because it is readily available and competitively priced, but mainly because of its pleasing rendering of colour right across the spectrum. For high-quality work which does not require a fast film, I use Fuji Velvia (ISO 50) for its very fine grain, its ability to resolve minute detail, and its vibrant colours. For day-to-day work it's Fuji Sensia ISO 100 with its softer colours and extra speed, but for photographing birds in flight or animals running quickly, I move up to Sensia 200 or 400 depending on the light level at the time. I occasionally 'push' the fast films by 1 stop but have never been completely satisfied with the results as there is usually some small loss of image quality and a slight colour shift. All the processing (E6) is done by a local professional laboratory in just over an hour, allowing me when necessary to make adjustments and reshoot, often on the same day.

REFLECTORS AND DIFFUSERS

Reflectors illuminate an area which would otherwise be underlit or in shadow. They vary in their reflective power; a mirror is a 100 per cent reflector which functions almost as a second main light, while crinkled aluminium cooking-foil produces a more diffused light. A plain white surface is a much weaker reflector delivering a very soft diffused lighting. I collect small reflectors from odd sources, including lids from Chinese take-away containers (white and silver), circular cake base-boards (crinkled silver and gold) and bathroom cabinet mirrors and ladies' compacts' mirrors (100 per cent reflective surfaces). You can of course buy professionally made white, silver and gold reflectors from Lastolite.

A diffuser is used to soften the light source. When the sunlight is bright and harsh, I often stretch a white handkerchief between the sun and the subject (close-up work) to soften the lighting and reduce the contrast. Flash lighting can produce hard-edged shadows and a handkerchief tied over the flash head will soften the light considerably but absorb at least 1 stop in the process.

CAMERA SUPPORTS

When using a long lens or working in close-up, one of the biggest problems is keeping the camera sufficiently rigid to prevent camera shake. The obvious solution is to use a tripod such as one of the Benbo range, which are very versatile and ideal for nature photography. The latest, very expensive but extremely strong carbon fibre tripods are, to my mind, too light, lacking the inertia necessary to keep them stable out of doors in anything other than completely windless conditions. Instead of the traditional ball-and-socket or pan-and-tilt head, I use a Manfrotto handgrip (or joystick) with its adjustable trigger-controlled, spring-loaded ball-and-socket base and quick-release camera fitting on top. Beanbags placed on a car roof or on a wall can be remarkably effective while a small camera clamp table tripod is worth a corner in anyone's camera bag. Monopods and shoulder pods give extra stability to a hand-held camera when photographing birds in flight or animals on the move. Whatever method you choose, an efficient camera support is essential if your images are to fulfil their sharpness potential.

The Benbo tripod is strong and versatile, extending up to 1.57m (62 in) with a unique construction allowing it to be used in water without damaging it.

SHUTTER RELEASE SYSTEMS

There is little point in setting up the camera on a firm tripod and then prodding the shutter button with an extended digit. Always use a cable or electric release, although the built-in timer is useful in an emergency. Other release methods which I have used include a long twin electrical cable and switch plugged into the Olympus autowinder, a 10m (33 ft) pneumatic release and a radio remote control consisting of a small hand-held transmitter and a camera-linked receiver, which is effective up to about 40m (130 ft). All these devices have their particular uses – it's a case of choosing the right one for the job – horses for courses.

FLASH EQUIPMENT

The benefits of electronic flash are almost too obvious to state: powerful, very short duration, daylight colour temperature and portability. A practical way to specify the power output of a flash unit without getting involved in joules or lumen seconds is to use the flash guide number, where the GN = f number x flash-to-subject distance in metres, using ISO 100/21° film. Thus, with a GN of 32 and a subject distance of 4 metres, the appropriate lens aperture would be f 8. Using the Olympus OM system, I originally bought their fairly powerful T32 flash units (GN 32 for ISO 100/21° film), but more recently I have started to use what is probably the world's most popular flash unit, the Metz Mecablitz 45 (GN 45 for ISO 100/21° film). Linked to the Metz SCA 300 adapters, the CL3 and 4 can be used in the fully automatic TTL mode on my Olympus, Minolta and Pentax 645N cameras. The Olympus T32 and the Metz unit can also be used in the automatic telecomputer and the manual modes but for 99 per cent of the time I use the TTL setting to ensure well exposed (most of the time) transparencies. Shutter synchronisation speeds of 1/60 or 1/125 second do lead occasionally to secondary ghost images, which is why some manufacturers produce at least one leaf-shutter lens, where the shutter blades are fully open, however briefly, on every shutter setting, providing perfect flash synchronisation right across the shutter speed range.

The Manfrotto handgrip or joystick has a trigger-operated spring-loaded ball-and-socket base with a quick-release camera fitting on top. It can be quickly set up in any position and is extremely rigid.

The combined G-clamp, miniature tripod and threaded spike is a very versatile gadget, seen here clamped to the handle of a wheelbarrow. The tripod legs and central spike have been screwed in place for the photograph. When using the clamp facility, they would be stored away in the clamp body.

TIPS ON BUYING EQUIPMENT

❖ Choose a 'systems' camera (e.g. Nikon, Canon, Minolta) with both manual and autofocus facilities. The 35mm format is by far the most popular, but the much more expensive medium format cameras (e.g. Bronica, Mamiya, Pentax) have a very loyal following.

❖ Look for the following: preview lever or button, cable release or electronic release socket and an exposure compensation button or switch – they are extremely useful devices but are not all present on all 35mm SLR cameras.

❖ 'Programme' mode exposure is totally inadequate for nature photography. You need at least aperture (or shutter) priority and full manual control.

❖ Buy the best quality lenses you can afford but only when you definitely need them. A 24 or 28mm is a good all-round wide angle lens, while a 50mm macro lens is more versatile than the standard 50mm lens, being able to focus from infinity right down to at least 1/2 life-size. A 90mm macro lens is a useful focal length when photographing small subjects such as flowers, bees, butterflies and small rodents.

❖ The best quality telephoto lenses are apochromatics (APOs). A 75–300mm, 400mm, and a 500 or 600mm lens will cover virtually anything you are likely to want to photograph. Independent lens manufacturers such as Sigma, Tokina and Tamron produce APO lenses which are less expensive than the camera manufacturers' lenses but are nevertheless of excellent quality. Add a good quality x1.4 or x2 teleconverter to your list – light and fairly inexpensive and very useful on occasions.

❖ Invest in good quality lens hoods, preferably with rectangular apertures. The bellow-type is quite expensive, but versatile and very effective – a good investment.

❖ As a nature photographer you will not need a bagful of filters – a polariser, amber warm-up and a graduated neutral density are the basic requirements.

❖ A heavy, good quality tripod (e.g. Benbo) is absolutely essential. I never work without one. Carbon-fibre tripods are very light and strong (and very expensive) but don't have sufficient inertia to withstand breezy weather conditions.

❖ You will need at least a couple of flash units. Buy fairly powerful (e.g. GN 32–40 on ISO 100 film) but not too bulky units from either the camera manufacturer or an independent such as Metz, with facilities to use them off the camera.

❖ Don't be afraid to buy second-hand cameras and lenses. Many amateurs (but not nature photographers of course!) change their equipment almost annually in a bid to keep up to date with the latest innovations. Much of this equipment is 'as new' but at a greatly reduced price. Most of my equipment (cameras, lenses, flash units and tripods) was bought second-hand and has always been trouble-free, or have I just been very lucky?

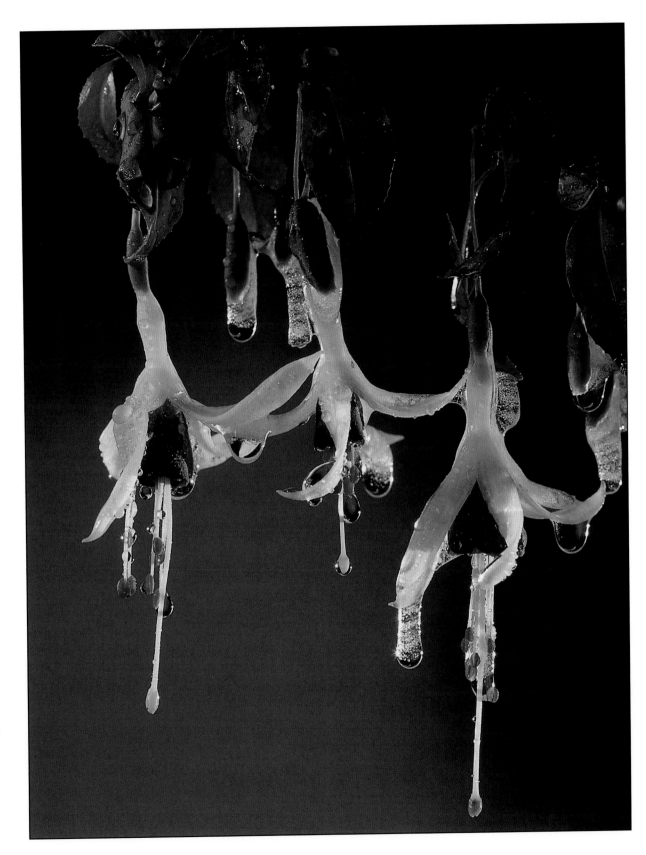

Rain and freezing conditions resulted in the fuschias becoming sheathed in ice. I brought a twig indoors and used backlit flash and a frontal reflector to light the flowers.

Mamiya 645, 80mm Macro lens, flash, f16, Fuji Provia 100.

CHAPTER THREE

Composition

Most people can recognise a 'good' or 'pleasing' picture without being able to say precisely what makes it good or pleasing. For some, good composition is instinctive and second nature, but for others it has to be explained and thought about before the concept becomes understood.

Composition refers to the way we visually arrange the various elements of the subject to form a harmonious whole. The final image might be dramatic, moody, pastoral or even jarring but if you are happy with the arrangement and treatment of the various elements, then for you the composition is satisfactory. Composition can be a very personal concept but for your work to be appreciated by a wider audience, then to some degree you should compose the image within guidelines which are universally accepted.

Analyse the paintings of Rembrandt, Turner and Monet, or the photographs of Karsh, Cartier-Bresson and Lichfield, or the wildlife images of Stephen Dalton, John Shaw and Laurie Campbell, and you will discover that they have all been very carefully composed, often along well-established lines. The 'rules' of composition are not meant to be a straightjacket, suppressing your own creativity but merely a guide, as you develop your own particular style. A successful picture is a combination of technical skills which can easily be mastered, and your aesthetic awareness which puts your own individual stamp on the image.

SELECTING THE SUBJECT

Your first task is to select the subject, which for a nature photographer might seem like stating the obvious. Is the aim to produce a large picture for hanging, to illustrate a magazine or book, as part of a lecture, or to send to a picture agency? Having decided on exactly what your objective is, you can then set about trying to achieve it.

PICTURE SHAPE AND BOUNDARIES

Generally speaking, the horizontal or landscape format is, as the name suggests, appropriate for many landscapes or any picture intended to convey peace and tranquillity, whereas the vertical or portrait format suggests imposing subjects like high buildings or tall natural objects such as a section of coniferous woodland or an avenue of Lombardy poplars. Close-ups of tall plants or sitting animals often look more effective in the portrait format, whereas animals moving across the field of view will fit the horizontal format much better. These suggestions can be discarded when the subject calls for a more radical approach.

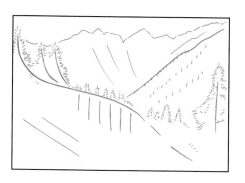

The horizontal format is appropriate for most landscapes. The third dimension, depth, is apparent because most of the indicators of perspective are present. The foreground is bold and dark-toned; the middle-distance wooded slopes are beginning to lose their colour and the distant mountains are a pastel greyish-blue. Exposure: 1/4 sec, f 22. 75mm lens (medium format). Fuji Velvia. Julian Alps, Slovenia.

Imposing buildings or tall natural objects such as conifer trees are often shown to advantage in the 'portrait' format, which concentrates the eye (and the mind) on the tallness of the trees rather than the overall horizontal landscape of which they are part. Exposure: 1 sec, f 16. Standard 90mm lens (6 x 7cm format). Fuji Provia 100.

The large piercing eyes and aggressive beak of the Great Horned Owl fit perfectly into the horizontal format forcing us to concentrate on these striking features.
Exposure: flash, f 16. 75–300mm lens. Kodak Elite 100.

Despite the undoubted popularity of the Hasselblad, Rollei and other 6 x 6cm format cameras, I have never been happy using the square format. Rarely did the viewfinder image look just right and I spent much time mentally cropping it to produce a horizontal or vertical format image. Why was this, and why are so few pictures in art galleries perfectly square? Is it linked to the 'Golden Section' or 'Golden Rectangle' where the ratio of the long side to the short one is 8:5 (or 1:0.63). Enlarging papers, such as the old postcard $5\frac{1}{2}$ x $3\frac{1}{2}$ in (14 x 9cm), have a ratio of 1:0.64, while whole plate, $8\frac{1}{2}$ x $6\frac{1}{2}$ in (22 x 16.5cm), and 16 x 12 in (41 x 30cm) papers have ratios of 1:0.76 and 1:0.75 respectively. The 35mm film format 36 x 24mm comes very close at 1:0.66, with the medium format 56 x 40mm producing a ratio of 1:0.7. I don't know if our attraction to this rectangular shape is cultural or inherent in our nature, but a ratio of around 1:0.7 seems to produce a satisfactory rectangular shape.

SUBJECT POSITION AND SIZE

The obvious place for the subject is right in the centre of the frame where it will have immediate impact. Unfortunately the interest is usually short-lived and eventually the image becomes quite boring. A way to avoid this is to move the subject towards the side of the frame in a position suggested by the 'rule of thirds'. You mentally divide the image area into thirds using imaginary horizontal and vertical lines and where the four lines intersect are the 'strong' points, near which the subject should be located. The rule of thirds is not a man-made rule but something inherent in the human psyche, being closely related to the 'Golden Section' and 'Golden Rectangle' mentioned earlier. It was probably known and used by the Egyptians some 5,000 years ago; it was certainly employed by the Greeks in their art and architecture and is still universally used today. Having located the animal or bird near one of the strong points, it is good practice to have it looking into the area of greatest space, because it 'looks right' and provides space for the animal to 'move' into.

The relative size of the animal or plant is also important, with 'large' not always producing the greatest impact. At the other extreme, too small a subject loses significance, becoming just a minor component of the total image.

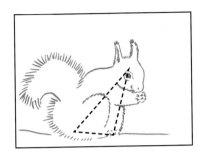

A triangle in a composition suggests stability and solidarity (unless balanced on one corner) but in this shot the triangle is leaning forward slightly introducing a degree of instability, which is counterbalanced by the weight of the squirrel's tail. Without the help of the large bushy tail, the squirrel would squat with its head and upper body pulled further back, producing a perfectly stable, triangular composition.
Exposure: 1/30sec, f5.6, 400mm lens, Kodak Elite 200.

EYE LINES AND IMAGE BALANCE

Eye lines are real or imaginary lines which lead the eye around the picture, consciously or subconsciously helping the brain to seek out and identify patterns and shapes. An obvious example is the curved line of a river which can lead the eye quite naturally through the picture taking in various points of interest before it ends on the horizon or disappears out of the frame.

A composition in which the main subject resembles a triangle suggests solidarity and stability, while a diagonal line or a triangle balanced on one corner implies instability, motion and dynamism. An 'L'-shaped configuration also suggests stability and is often used to frame a landscape, while an inverted 'U' is frequently utilised in the form of a stone arch or overhanging foliage to frame a scene and give it stability.

If you want an image to feel balanced, a large area of light colour should be counterbalanced by something smaller and more dense or larger and lighter, on the other side. The composition of a picture is often linked to the camera angle and position, so that a low camera position will not only enhance the immediate foreground and reduce the middle distance, but will also allow small nearby objects to stand out more dramatically. A higher camera position results in a field of view similar to that seen by a man standing upright and although this is often used (more by default than for any specific reason!), it is not necessarily the most appropriate position. Pointing the camera vertically down can result in yet another interesting viewpoint when photographing, for example, a barnacle-covered rock or crocuses in a garden border.

COLOUR

Images which are predominantly one colour evoke a particular emotional response often associated with these colours in the natural world. For example, yellows and reds are associated with sunsets, inducing feelings of warmth and even intense heat, while

The natural unadulterated colours of the trees, rape flowers and grass are brought together to form a well-composed, harmonious image. Normally a completely cloudless blue sky would be avoided but in this context it fits in well with the other elements of the picture. The path below the trees leads the eye gently through the scene, helped by the decreasing tree size which adds a sense of perspective. On the negative side, the distant telegraph poles are a small annoyance. Exposure: 1/30 sec, f 22. 90mm lens. Fuji Velvia.

blue, the colour of sky and water, is a 'clean' but 'cool' colour implying peace and tranquillity. Blue-grey is a cold colour, which is strikingly effective in winter scenes where it creates an atmosphere of cold desolation. Green is a restful colour associated with grass and trees, promoting feelings of space and calm. It is also a 'receding' colour, making it useful as a non-distracting background in close-up work, while certain shades of red are 'advancing' colours which seem to lift themselves off the page.

Colour saturation (in photography) refers to the intensity or 'richness' of the colours. Unsaturated colours are pastel shades; fully saturated colours are strong and vibrant. To create softer-toned colours, if not already present in the scene, most photographers change the film speed setting to slightly overexpose the film. A classic example is Fuji Velvia slide film, which at its rated value of ISO 50 produces rich 'punchy' colours, but when exposed at ISO 40 (a favoured alternative), the results are softer and more appropriate for certain subjects.

PATTERNS AND SYMMETRY

Pattern, like rhythm, is based on repetition, allowing the eye to roam freely across the image, engendering a feeling of

predictability and even restfulness. Other patterns, such as the bark of a tree or a canopy of autumn leaves, are random, but when a small area is carefully isolated it too can be attractive, well composed and balanced for colour and tone.

Some patterns are based on radial symmetry, with the elements spreading out from a central point as seen in many flowers such as daisies, dandelions and ragwort, and in a few marine creatures like starfish, sea anemones and sea urchins. The centre of the pattern would normally be placed at one of the strong points in the frame, but occasionally the 'rule of thirds' can be broken by locating it right in the centre, emphasising the perfect radial symmetry of the organism. (Patterns and abstract images are discussed in more detail in the final chapter.)

LIGHTING

The atmosphere and general appeal of a picture is influenced greatly by the lighting, which at the extremes can be either hard and unyielding or soft and subtle, each creating its own effect on the subject. Harsh light is emitted from a point source, resulting in high contrast lighting with dark sharp-edged shadows, as typified by the midday sun in a clear blue sky or the concentrated beam

An abstract pattern produced by a mixture of textures and colours in this long-dead sweet chestnut tree. Exposure: 1/30 sec, f 16. 50mm macro lens. Kodak Elite 50.

from a slide projector. This type of lighting is shunned by most photographers because the contrast is too high and the shadows too blocked up.

As the light source increases in diameter, the shadows become more soft-edged, as seen when a point-source flash is fired into a flash umbrella. The size of the light source is equal to the area of the 'brolly' flash, resulting in softer lighting with more detail in the shadows. On a completely overcast day, the sky is an unbroken hemisphere of flat diffused light with no shadows at all, which for obvious reasons is not ideal for most photographic work (except, possibly, close-up photography).

Frontal lighting, whether harsh or diffused, is 'safe' lighting because everything facing the camera will be clearly lit, hence the advice given to amateur photographers to keep the sun behind them. Unfortunately frontal lighting is very flat and rather uninteresting, producing no modelling or three-dimensional effects. But when the main light is in the 45° frontal position, i.e. 45° above and 45° to one side, it creates good modelling, which may or may not require a small fill-in light or reflector to lighten the darker shadows.

Other useful types of lighting are grazing (or low oblique) which emphasises surface texture and is employed extensively in both landscape and close-up photography. Backlighting is favoured by many nature photographers (including myself), where the main light is behind and usually above the subject and directed towards the camera. It works well in animals and plants fringed with delicate hairs or fine bristles, with the ability to transform an average subject into something quite special. As the light is shining almost directly into the camera lens you will need to use an efficient light shield such as a conventional lens hood or a piece of card (or your hand) held just out of the picture area, shading the lens from direct sunlight.

DEPTH AND PERSPECTIVE

You can produce an illusion of depth in a two-dimensional photograph by applying some of the principles of monocular (or single-point) perspective. For example, if a photograph depicts two objects of similar size but at different distances from the camera, the nearer one will be larger than the more distant one. Although this may seem obvious to us, in early paintings the larger the object the more powerful it was deemed to be, regardless of where it was placed in the picture.

Above: A regularly repeated, almost symmetrical pattern engenders a feeling of stability and organisation. Exposure: 1/60 sec, f 8. 50mm macro lens. Kodak Elite 100.

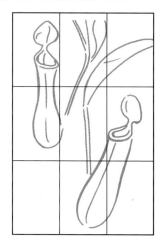

The pitcher plant, Nepenthes, is a native of New Guinea, with each pitcher containing an acidic juice, sufficiently strong to kill and digest any hapless creature which inadvertently falls into it.
Both pitchers are located at strong points in the frame (see diagram) where the 'thirds' intersect, resulting in a well-balanced and interesting composition. Exposure: 1/4 sec, f 16. 90mm macro lens. Fuji Velvia.

Another way of generating depth in a picture is to include some form of linear perspective, where parallel lines, such as the banks of a canal, converge towards the horizon. Similarly if the camera is pointing vertically upwards in a forest, the tree trunks converge towards some unspecified point in the sky.

Colour changes can also help to impart a feeling of depth and atmosphere to a photograph. Due to atmospheric haze produced by moisture and dust particles in the air, faraway objects slowly lose their strong colours which are replaced by pastel-shade greys and blues. Definition also suffers as distant hills and mountains look much less distinct than those in the near and middle distance. In regions with crystal clear, haze-free atmospheres, the 'depth' effect is completely lost with everything from the near distance to the horizon being sharp, clear and full of colour but completely flat and two-dimensional. It is worth remembering that a wide-angle lens stretches the perspective producing exaggerated depth while a telephoto lens has the opposite effect.

Right: The third dimension, depth, is apparent because some of the indicators of perspective are present. The foreground is bold, dark-toned and clearly defined, with the more distant trees losing their tone as they fade into the late afternoon mist. The snow-dusted path carries the eye through the scene before vanishing into the mist. Exposure: 1/4 sec, f16. 50mm lens.

Overleaf: The same indicators of depth and perspective are present but the winter mist has been replaced by a summer heat haze. Exposure: 1/60 sec, f22, Fuji Provia 100.

Aysgarth Upper Falls, Yorkshire Dales, in spring. The foreground leaves and branches form a natural frame to the picture, producing a feeling of depth and drawing the viewer into the scene. Note how the backlit sycamore leaves along the top of the frame are highlighted against the dark unlit wooded area on the far side.
Exposure: 1/125 sec, f 8. 75mm lens (6 x 4.5cm format). Fuji Provia 100.

TIPS ON COMPOSITION

❖ An oil painting may take weeks or even months to complete and at each stage the painter is in control of the various elements of the composition. A photograph can be taken in 1/60 second – a mere 'blink of an eye' on the painter's time-scale – and because photographs can be taken so quickly, there is a tendency to do just that; this should be avoided at all costs.

❖ Plan the composition of the image in detail long before the shutter is released. Visit a potential photographic site several times to study the direction of the light and to check the stage of development of plants, trees or newly hatched chicks.

❖ Consider the choice of lens and whether a wide-angle view or the shortened perspective and larger image of a telephoto lens would best suit your purposes.

❖ Close-up photographs of animals and plants may require extra lighting, while some backgrounds must be rendered sharp to provide additional information and others thrown well out of focus to be non-distracting.

❖ Spend time thinking about what exactly you are trying to achieve.

❖ Study the image in the viewfinder of the hand-held camera, moving a few metres to either side and trying different camera heights before making the final decision.

❖ Mount the camera firmly on a tripod and adjust the height, lens aperture (depth of field) and overall exposure, before finally releasing the shutter.

❖ Very occasionally something very interesting crops up, for example a sparrow hawk diving on an unsuspecting pigeon, leaving you no time to actively consider camera angles and composition. Use the 'point and shoot' technique which can often be successful because with practice and experience composition becomes instinctive.

CHAPTER FOUR

The World in Close-up

A great deal of nature photography is done at distances much closer than the standard lens can focus, which is about 45cm (18in). The area covered is a little larger than A4 size, producing an image one-eighth (1:8) life-size. Many animals and plants are much smaller than this and, although magnified images can be very exciting, there are problems which increase dramatically with the degree of magnification. In this chapter we shall be dealing with magnifications ranging from x1 (life-size) right up to x400, the latter being the province of the compound microscope.

The chief areas to be looked at are the choice of lens and lens attachments, vibration, illumination, exposure determination and depth of field.

LENSES FOR CLOSE-UP PHOTOGRAPHY

The easiest and cheapest way of producing a larger, but still sharp, image is to screw a close-up (or supplementary) lens onto the front of the standard lens. This shortens the focal length, allowing the camera closer to the subject, while still keeping it in sharp focus. These lenses come in strengths of 1, 2, 3 etc. dioptres (the reciprocal of the focal length in metres) and are basically the same as +1, +2 D etc. spectacle lenses for reading. For example, a 3-dioptre close-up lens (focal length 1/3 metre, 33cm) on a camera lens set at its closest focusing distance (45cm) will focus down to 27cm, covering an area slightly smaller than a postcard (14 x 9 cm).

The majority are uncorrected single-element lenses, which produce reasonably satisfactory results when the camera lens is stopped well down so that only the central portion of the close-up lens is being used. Some manufacturers such as Nikon, Zeiss, Sigma and Olympus supply two-element achromatic doublets as close-up lenses for their standard and zoom lenses, and these are well worth having.

REVERSED LENSES

A technique which I first saw described by John Shaw, the well-known American nature photographer, involves the use of 'stacked' lenses where, for example, a standard 50mm lens functions as a highly corrected close-up lens when reversed onto a 135 or 200mm telephoto lens. The magnification produced by this combination is calculated by dividing the focal length of the prime lens by that of the lens reversed onto it; a 200mm f 4 lens used with a 50mm f 1.8 will produce a magnification of 200 ÷ 50 = x4. This method is worth trying but you will have to make your own adapter ring using two empty filter mounts (one for each lens) glued together face-to-face.

A Tamron 90mm macro lens was used to photograph this oriental poppy, Papaver orientale. Note the superb sharpness of the image aided by using flash (1/1000 sec exposure) and fine grain film. Exposure: flash, f11, –1 stop underexposure. 90mm macro lens. Kodak Ektrachrome 64.

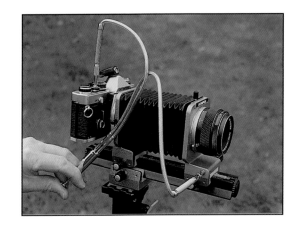

A bellows unit is very useful when taking close-ups larger than half life-size, and essential with macro lenses which do not have built-in focusing. The double cable release synchronises the lens diaphragm operation with the camera shutter release.

A final method of getting closer is to reverse the standard 50mm lens onto the camera body, via extension tubes or a bellows unit, using an adapter, when the definition can be quite excellent particularly at higher magnifications. A good quality enlarging lens used on a bellows unit produces superb results in the normal and reversed positions. The iris diaphragm will have to be set and used manually which can be a slight disadvantage.

EXTENSION TUBES AND BELLOWS UNITS

Yet another way of obtaining a larger but still sharp image is to move the standard lens further away from the film and nearer to the subject (this happens in all macro lenses). It can be done with extension tubes (manual or automatic), which are usually available in sets of three, or by using a bellows unit (again manual or automatic) which performs the same function but is quicker and easier to use. A final method of increasing the image size is to use a teleconverter – this was discussed in the previous chapter.

MACRO LENSES

Most manufacturers produce at least one macro lens, which is optically corrected for high quality close-up work by incorporating a 'floating' lens element in the design, but will also function as a normal lens and focus at infinity. Macro lenses have a very flat field (which makes them ideal for document copy work), with built-in extension allowing them to focus down to life-size without resorting to extension tubes.

Olympus make a whole raft of macro lenses from the 20 and 38mm f3.5 with their RMS standard 20mm diameter microscope thread, the ever popular 50mm f2 and f3.5, to the 80mm f4 and the 135mm f4.5. While the 50mm lens has in-built focusing from infinity down to half life-size, the others are lens heads, requiring a bellows unit or the Olympus telescopic autotube. Magnifications up to x12 are available, with each lens producing its best performance over a limited specified range.

Macro lenses are very high quality optics, but excellence does not come cheaply with at least a threefold increase in price over the same focal length non-macro lens and usually a loss of two stops of light at maximum aperture.

VIBRATION

In extreme close-up work, the slightest movement of the camera or subject during the exposure can result in a blurred image. Even the vibration caused by a free-standing electric fan heater or passing traffic can soften the image, which is the main reason why electron microscopes are housed in deep basements. If you have ever seen photographs of the huge camera rigs and gantries used by Oxford Scientific Films or the BBC Natural History Unit at Bristol, you will appreciate just how important rigidity is in the quest for super-sharp images.

Opposite: Using a medium format Pentax 645N camera this close-up image of a Passion flower could only be achieved by coupling a matched X2 converter and a 2-element close-up lens to the Pentax 120mm macro lens. Daylight illumination. Exposure: 3 sec, effective aperture f32, Fuji Velvia 50.

Close-up of an orchid using the Olympus 80mm f4 macro lens mounted on a bellows unit. Focusing was done by moving the lens, bellows and camera body as one unit, with the helicoid fine focusing built into the lens head used to fine-tune the sharpness of the image. Exposure: 4 sec, f22. 80mm macro lens. Kodak Ektachrome 64. Singapore.

ILLUMINATION

The problem of lighting for close-up work is that you just can't get sufficient of it. The main reason is the Inverse Square Law of Illumination, which states that as the lens is moved further away from the film surface (as in close-up work), the intensity of the illumination decreases, not in direct proportion to the distance but to the square of the distance. For example, if the lens (and bellows) is extended to three times the normal working distance from the film surface, the light level on the film will not be a third, but one-ninth of its former value. And as the magnification reaches x10, the light level falls to 1/121 of its original value which presents formidable lighting problems in all but completely static material.

The chief types of illumination used in close-up work are daylight, tungsten lamps and electronic flash. Most field photography is done using daylight, which on a clear cloudless day is highly directional as the sun is effectively a point source. A lightly overcast sky produces a softer, more diffused light with lower contrast, while a heavy leaden sky results in very flat, shadowless lighting. Though the sunlight may look quite bright, it might not be sufficiently strong when working at life-size (or greater) where, due to the Inverse Square Law, a fourfold or more increase in exposure will be required.

COLOUR TEMPERATURE

Light changes colour during the day and this can be defined in terms of colour temperature measured in Kelvins (K), where 0 (zero) K is the same as −273°C (absolute zero) or, put another way, Kelvin temperature (K) = Celsius temperature (°C) + 273.

The colour emitted by a hot non-reflective object (a so-called 'black body radiator') bears a simple relationship to its temperature in

The shore barnacle, Balanus balanoides, magnified x5, using a 20mm f 3.5 Zuiko macro lens, stopped down to its minimum aperture of f 16 (effective aperture f 96).
To supply the large amount of light required, a Metz 45 flash unit was positioned 15cm (6in) above and behind the barnacles with a T32 flash unit as a frontal light.

Kelvins. As the temperature rises, the black body emits first red, then yellow, white, and finally bluish light, increasing from 1,500 to around 15,000 K. The colour of spring sunlight with white reflectiveclouds is very similar to the black body at a temperature of 5,500K, this being the standard to which all daylight colour films are balanced. On the same scale, electronic flash also has a colour temperature of around 5,500K, which is why it is often referred to as 'portable sunlight'. Photofloods and tungsten halogen lamps register temperatures of around 3,400K, while a candle flame with its distinctly red-yellow light brings up the rear at 1,500K.

The colour temperature of light varies throughout the day with a low 1,500–3,000K at sunrise and sunset (assuming a fairly cloudless sky) and a high 5,500K at midday, while a clear blue sky can register a lofty 15,000K (almost violet). When the colour temperature of the light does not match the film, a colour bias will be present, with the glorious sunset (2,000K) looking overly red, although most photographers are more than happy to leave it uncorrected.

Blue and amber filters raise or lower respectively the colour temperature of light passing through them and are designated according to their 'strength' or mired shift (a mired is 1 million divided by the colour temperature). As mentioned in the previous chapter, I occasionally use a pale amber 81C 'warm-up' filter on outdoor scenes and a pale blue filter on my hand-held video light.

Light Source	Colour Temperature Kelvin (K)	Conversion Filter for Daylight-balanced film	Exposure Increase
Blue northern sky	10,000–15,000	amber 85B	2/3
Cloudy day	7,500	amber 81B	1/3
Sun at midday	5,500	none	–
Electronic flash	5,500	none	–
Photoflood lamp	3,400	blue 80B	1 2/3
Quartz halogen lamp	3,200	blue 80A	2
Sunset	1,500–3,000	blue 80A	2
Candle light	1,500	blue 80A and 80B	3 2/3

ARTIFICIAL LIGHT

I rarely use artificial lighting as the main source of illumination in close-up work because it produces too much heat (a heat filter of infrared-absorbing glass is required), it does not concentrate the light onto a sufficiently small area unless a small spotlight or slide projector is used and it requires a strong 80A blue filter (which absorbs 2 stops of light) to raise the colour temperature up to daylight, (unless film balanced for artificial light is used).

However, I quite often use a small hand-held video light as a modelling light when working outdoors in dull weather or indoors where the ambient daylight is often too flat. When two pieces of pale-blue acetate sheet are fastened over the light, the colour temperature approximates daylight. I have little choice but to use the built-in tungsten lighting when examining material under the microscope although I frequently use flash for the actual photographs – this is discussed later in the chapter.

FLASH LIGHTING

Electronic flash has been aptly called 'portable sunlight', with characteristics which make it arguably the best source of lighting for close-up work. Physically small units such as the Olympus T20 and T32 can be positioned really close to the subject without any fear of 'frying' it, as they remain quite cold, while their high output allows you to use small lens apertures with a welcome increase in the depth of field. The very short flash duration of at least 1/1000 second is sufficient to 'freeze' the movement of most small creatures and the daylight colour temperature permits the use of daylight-balanced film without having to resort to colour correction filters.

I have several small but quite powerful flash units linked to the camera through TTL leads, with the camera's off-the-film (OTF) flash metering system determining the exposures, although I do bracket them when dealing with 'tricky' subjects. Without TTL leads, the flash could be triggered by slave units but exposure determination would be a problem, requiring a series of test exposures.

The only disadvantage of using flash is that you cannot predict with any certainty the final result of the lighting arrangement. I often use the hand-held video light to find the best lighting set-up, later replacing it with the flash units. When working in a tight space, a ring-flash attached to the lens barrel can be useful, providing shadowless, if somewhat flat, lighting. As all 35mm SLR cameras have focal plane shutters with a flash synchronisation speed of 1/60 or 1/125 second, there is always the possibility of ghost images if the subject is moving and the ambient light level is high.

EXPOSURE DETERMINATION

The f-numbers on a lens are correct only when the lens is focused near infinity and as the lens is moved further away from the film plane in close-up work, the level of illumination decreases in accordance with the Inverse Square Law. These longer than normal distances can be allowed for by applying the following simple formula:

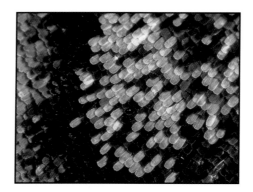

Peacock butterfly, Inachis io, wing, showing the alignment of the scales. Photographed through the microscope using a x3 objective and x10 eyepiece, producing x30 magnification. Grazed surface lighting was supplied by two Metz 45s, 10cm (4in) away.

Effective f-number = Marked f-number x (Magnification + 1)

Thus in close-up work where the magnification might be, for example, x3, a marked (or set) f-number of f 8 becomes an effective or functional f-number of 8 x (3 + 1) = 32, illustrating quite clearly why such high light levels are necessary when photographing living material in close-up. If your camera is equipped with OTF flash metering, exposure determination is not a problem; if not, trial exposures will be necessary as the flash unit's automatic setting does not take account of changes from marked to effective f-numbers.

Magnification x life-size	Multiply f-number by	Exposure Increase
1/20	1.05	1.1
1/10	1.1	1.21
1/5	1.2	1.44
1/2	1.5	2.25
life-size	2	4
2	3	9
4	5	25
10	11	121

DEPTH OF FIELD

As the camera moves closer to the subject and the magnification increases, the depth of field becomes increasingly shallow. Using a 50mm lens at f4 and focused at 1 metre (39 in), the depth of field is a reasonable 8 cm (3 in), but when focused at 25 cm (10 in) it is a mere 0.95 cm (0.37 in). If the same lens is then focused really close to produce x5 magnification, the depth of field is reduced to a microscopic 0.007 cm (0.003 in) and even when stopped down to f16 it is still only 0.023 cm (0.01 in). Critical focusing is therefore essential. At high magnifications it is much easier to focus accurately if you set the bellows to the magnification required and

A large tropical swallowtail butterfly resting between visits to flowers for nectar. A 90 mm macro lens produced a reasonably large image without getting too close. Exposure: 1/60 sec, f16. 90 mm macro lens. Kodak Elite 100. Offshore island, Singapore.

move the entire camera/bellows combination using a focusing stage until the subject is sharp. You can then fine-focus the image using the bellows movement, or the fine focusing built into the lens head (some have it) or even by very slightly screwing or unscrewing the lens.

PHOTOMICROGRAPHY

If you want to produce a highly magnified image of a water flea, a butterfly's antenna, or a cluster of finely sculptured pollen grains, the ultimate magnifier is the compound microscope. With it any competent photographer can take photographs not only of static material, but living moving creatures. To the casual observer, the microscope probably looks quite complicated, but basically it is nothing more than a powerful magnifier with an illumination and focusing system added to it.

The final magnification is the product of the magnifying power of the objective lens and the eyepiece lens. The former is the main magnifier and is available from x2.5 to x100, while the eyepiece, which is much simpler optically, is available in three popular magnifications, x5, x10, and x16.

The diameters and threads of eyepieces and objectives are standardised with products from different manufacturers being fully compatible. For nature photographers the lower magnifications, e.g. x2.5 to x40 objectives and x5 and x10 eyepieces are most useful, giving final magnifications ranging from x12.5 to x400.

On simpler microscopes the illumination is provided by daylight reflected from an adjustable substage mirror up through the optics into the eye. If daylight is too weak or unavailable, a small-wattage lamp can be used as a separate unit or built into the base of the microscope, the latter making the mirror redundant. A further refinement is a substage condenser lens (Abbe condenser) to concentrate the light onto the specimen. Finally, a substage iris diaphragm controls the aperture of the objective lens (and hence the depth of field) and the overall light intensity.

In comparison to cameras and lenses, microscopes are not expensive, with prices starting as low as £100, although for anyone seriously interested in photomicrography £350–£450 would buy a useful microscope with three objectives, two eyepieces, an Abbe condenser and built-in illumination (see Appendix for suppliers).

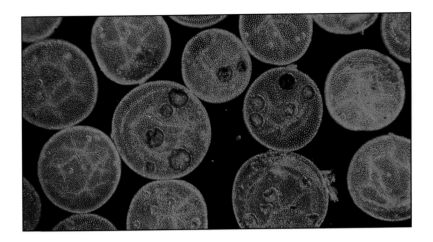

Volvox colonies with darkfield illumination, using a x3 objective and a x10 eyepiece, producing x30 magnification. The microscope's built-in illumination was used with suitable blue and green filtration to remove the yellow cast produced by the tungsten lighting (further details in chapter ten). Exposure: 6 sec. Fuji Sensia 100.

METHODS OF PHOTOMICROGRAPHY

Taking photographs through a microscope is quite easy using a 35mm SLR camera, as the only additional equipment required is a simple tube and a T2 adapter to link the camera body (minus the lens) to the microscope. Some microscope heads have an extra vertical tube specifically for photographic work, enabling you to use the microscope in the normal way and switch to the camera to take photographs.

Although any form of tungsten lighting can be used, the illumination will be insufficient to arrest the movement of living organisms. My technique is to use the built-in tungsten lighting to examine and focus the material, but use flash to make the exposure. You can do this by positioning a small half-silvered mirror (resembles smoked glass) at 45°, just above the light source with the flash unit next to it pointing horizontally. Much of the flash output is lost through and around the mirror but sufficient is reflected up into the microscope to produce well-exposed images and 'freeze' the movement of living organisms.

Flash units can also be positioned just above the stage to provide low-angle incident lighting but, as the substage iris diaphragm is not in use, the objective lens will be working fully 'open' with an even shallower depth of field. If your camera has OTF flash metering, exposure problems will be minimal, otherwise it means logging each exposure and selecting the best one after the film has been processed. The photomicrography of pond-life is discussed in Chapter 8, 'Ponds and Rivers'.

SUMMARY AND RECOMMENDATIONS

❖ The easiest and cheapest way to produce a close-up image is to screw a simple close-up lens onto the front of the standard lens. For slightly better results consider buying the more expensive two-element lenses (Nikon, Zeiss, Sigma, Olympus).

❖ Another method is to reverse the standard lens (via an adapter) onto a bellows unit or extension tube. You will lose any connections to the camera body, e.g. automatic diaphragm and sometimes the metering.

❖ You can also produce a larger image by moving the lens further away from the camera body by using an extension tube or bellows unit. Both are readily available in manual and auto versions.

❖ For serious close-up work there is nothing to beat a genuine macro lens, which will focus straight down to x1/2 life-size or even life-size. Unfortunately it costs up to four times more than a non-macro lens of the same focal length and is often two stops slower. A 90mm macro lens is an extremely useful and versatile optic.

❖ One of the biggest problems in close-up photography is vibration, with the effects becoming more obvious as the magnification increases. Always use a substantial tripod on a firm surface and trigger the shutter using a cable or electric release or the self-timer mechanism on the camera (where appropriate).

❖ Shortage of light is always a problem in close-up work, particularly when using a long bellows extension (remember the Inverse Square Law!), requiring more powerful lighting or much longer exposures (x2 life-size magnification requires 9x normal exposure).

❖ Powerful lighting from a spotlight or video light must be blue-filtered to raise its colour temperature (3,400 K) to around daylight levels (5,500 K). Heat production is also a problem.

❖ Flash lighting is powerful, cool and balanced for daylight, making it ideal for close-up work. The only disadvantage is you are working 'blind', making it very difficult to predict where the highlights and shadows will fall, but you can check the set-up using a hand-held video light.

❖ In close-up work as the magnification increases the depth of field decreases; at life-size magnification it can be less than 2 millimetres.

❖ If close-up work fascinates you, why not go a stage further, buy a microscope and enjoy the sheer beauty of the micro-world. A decent quality, quite versatile microscope can cost no more than the price of a 300 mm APO lens (around £450). You can pay a lot more of course, but good quality second-hand units are readily available (see Appendix).

The seahorse, Hippocampus kuda, is a small marine creature up to 5" (125mm) long which swims in the vertical position by undulations of the dorsal fin. Photographed, swimming in a seawater tank, using a 120mm macro lens. Exposure: flash, f16, Pentax 645, Fuji Velvia.

CHAPTER FIVE

Cliffs and Seashore

The coastline of England and Wales is approximately 2,700 miles (4,300 km) long with Scotland adding at least another 4,000 miles (6,400 km). On the east and south coast the rock is predominantly soft and weathers easily, with large areas being lost to the sea each year. Towards the far west, the rocks at Land's End are made of granites, with the hard rock continuing up the west coast to the hard red sandstones of north-west Scotland. The soft east coast rocks give way to hard rock as you approach the Farne Islands in Northumberland. The cliffs and offshore islands, particularly in the north and west, house some of the most magnificent seabird colonies in Europe including the majority of the world's population of razorbills and gannets.

Below the cliffs lies the seashore: an area of tremendous photographic potential, much neglected by nature photographers. Most of the plants are seaweeds (algae), many being unique to this environment, while a few species which can tolerate wide variations in salinity can penetrate several miles up tidal rivers. The animals inhabiting the seashore are mainly small invertebrates with sea urchins, starfish, sea squirts, jellyfish, sea anemones and limpets being unique to this area.

There is a high and low water twice every lunar day (24 hr 50 min) with the high tide moving forward 35–60 minutes each 24-hour day. Superimposed on this daily rhythm is a monthly rhythm of alternating spring and neap tides, two of each per lunar (28 days) month, with the maximum spring tides occurring approximately two days after each new and full moon. Finally a seasonal rhythm produces extra large spring tides during the March and September equinoxes, when the sun and moon are directly in line with the earth resulting in a maximum pull.

TYPES OF SHORE

There are four kinds of shore: rock, shingle, sand, and mud, and any shore could be a combination of these. Each shore has its own characteristics, but for photographic work the rocky shore is the most rewarding. The rocks form a solid base to which the seaweeds become attached, resulting in a luxuriant plant population able to support a wide range of animals. Rock pools, which are a distinctive feature of rocky shores, abound in a rich variety of flora and fauna, often making them the most rewarding of all the shore habitats.

Lundy Island, a high flat-topped piece of hard granite at the entrance to the Bristol Channel, 19 km (12 miles) NW of Hartland Point, Devon, England. During the breeding season it houses large colonies of seabirds, including Manx shearwater and puffins. It is now a National Trust sanctuary and the first British marine reserve. Exposure: 1/60 sec, f 8. 50mm lens. Kodak Gold ISO 100.

'A rolling stone gathers no moss.' Large rocks and pebbles which are constantly rolled about by the tides crush any plant life trying to establish itself. No plants also means no animals. Exposure: 1/125 sec, f 16. 35–135mm lens. Kodak Elite 100. Island of Pulau Tioman, Malaysia.

SEAWEEDS

Before going to the coast to take photographs, always check the tide times, trying to arrive at least one hour before low water, especially if you hope to photograph large kelps or sea urchins.

After arriving on the shore, I spent some time looking for good examples of the knotted wrack which were neither damaged by wave action nor nibbled by small marine creatures. Most seaweeds are best photographed out of water but if they are too dry they look quite dead. Some specimens looked healthy even though they were just beginning to dry out. This was good because a very wet surface produces a lot of unwanted reflections. During my first visit the weather was dry but overcast, resulting in flat lighting, but on a subsequent outing the sun shone brightly from a clear blue sky.

The tripod-mounted camera was set up over the seaweed with the film plane parallel to it to ensure edge-to-edge sharpness. Several shots were taken with the 90mm macro lens, which offered a reasonable working distance, using a cable release to operate the shutter. Always use a tripod, inconvenient though it often is, when exposures are longer than 1/60 sec. It will help to prevent camera shake. Just before the tide turned, I moved right down the shore to extreme low water to photograph the large kelp among the deep-water gullies and channels and, as the weather was dull and overcast, it was quite daunting and even a little frightening. Several exposures were made before retreating back up the shore.

On another occasion I took photographs of the same area but the sun was shining and the sky was blue – peaceful and not in the least scary. Photographing seaweeds can prove an interesting pursuit, well within the grasp of any keen nature photographer. As the interest grows, a photo-diary can be kept showing selected seaweeds at different seasons of the year. A particular shore can be photographed from the cliffs over several years to show the change in distribution of various plants and animals. For example, from above, brown and green seaweeds are easily identified as are barnacle-covered rocks and mussel beds (dirty white and black respectively).

The laminaria zone photographed at extreme low water captures the eerie atmosphere on a dark, forbidding day. The greyness of the sky is reflected in the water, adding to the drabness of the seaweeds. Exposure: 1/30 sec, ƒ8. 50mm lens. Kodak Elite 100.

EQUIPMENT

OLYMPUS OM2n

24, 50 AND 90MM LENSES,
POLARISING FILTER, TRIPOD,

CABLE RELEASE,

KODAK ELITE 100 FILM.

*Taken on a bright day with a hazy sun
reflecting some light from the surface
of the laminaria fronds.
A wide-angle lens was used to obtain
a close-up of the seaweeds but also to
show their background environment.
The diagonal line of the fronds leads
the eye from the bottom left up into
the centre where the large red-algae-
covered rocks stand out quite clearly.
Exposure: 1/125 sec, f 8. 35mm lens.
Kodak Elite 100.*

*The egg wrack photographed in
September on a dull overcast day
in diffused, rather flat lighting.
Characteristic of this seaweed are
the air bladders, with the red alga,
Polysiphonia fastigiata, always
associated with it. The diagonal
arrangement across the frame adds
interest to the composition, with the
fronds and air bladders cut by the
frame edge suggesting a continuous
spread of seaweed. Exposure: 1/30
sec, f 16. 90mm macro lens.
Kodak Elite 100.*

TIPS

❖ Study the weather forecast
before leaving home.

❖ Check the time of low water
(not high water).

❖ Take the minimum photo-
gear – it becomes heavier
the longer you have to carry
it on the shore.

❖ Wear plenty of warm
clothing. It's usually quite
cold, particularly at low
water with an onshore
breeze.

SEA URCHINS & STARFISH

Location Workshop

When the tide is out, sea urchins and starfish look quite dead but when covered by the incoming tide they become 'alive'. The aim of this assignment is to try to capture something of the 'aliveness' of these curious animals, which means photographing them underwater.

Echinoderms (hedgehog-skinned) are found only in the marine environment, and include sea urchins, starfish, brittle stars and the less well-known sea cucumbers and feather stars.

The common sea urchin, Echinus esculentus, lives in cool water among the rocks and kelp at extreme low water right down into the deeper sublittoral zone. Interesting features of the sea urchin include its five-point radial symmetry, which is clearly visible when the tube feet are extended, and the water circulatory system which controls the five double rows of tube feet, extending them only when the urchin is underwater. It uses the sucker-like tips to cling onto rock surfaces and as a very effective method of moving the urchin along the rocks. The urchin has a large mouth on the underside of the shell, surrounded by a complex five-toothed structure called 'Aristotle's lantern' which helps in the feeding process.

The common starfish, Asterias rubens, is found on the lower shore and is also built on a five-point radial symmetry as demonstrated by its five arms. Tube feet are present, being used for movement and feeding. The starfish is partial to mussels, which it forces open by attaching the tube feet and arms to the two halves of the shell. Should a starfish lose an arm to a larger predator, it has the unique ability to grow a new one.

Sea urchin photographed underwater showing the delicate extended tube feet. The urchin is positioned just off centre to make a more interesting composition while the surrounding fronds of green (Fucus vesiculosis) and red seaweed (Corallina officianalis) made a suitable frame. The deeper water behind the urchin has registered quite dark, allowing it, and in particular the delicate tube feet, to stand out. Exposure: 1/15 sec, f16. 90mm macro lens. Fuji Velvia.

EQUIPMENT

OLYMPUS OM2n

90MM MACRO LENS

TRIPOD

KODAK ELITE 100

FUJI VELVIA.

The starfish 'righting' itself by extending its tube feet, which grip the rock surface and slowly begin to turn the creature over. The tube feet work in a co-ordinated way with the fully extended ones indicating the direction of travel. The only other discernible change is that one of the periwinkles on the left side has moved out of frame between the two exposures. Exposure: 1/30 sec, f 16. 90mm macro lens. Kodak Elite 100.

TIPS

❖ Sand is very abrasive – don't photograph on a windy day.

❖ Use a skylight or UV filter to protect your lens from the salty atmosphere.

❖ Don't leave your equipment on a rock as you search for animals to photograph – you probably won't be able to find it again.

❖ Wear footwear with a 'grippy' sole – wet seaweeds are notoriously slippery.

I arrived on the rocky shore about an hour before low water and made my way down to the water's edge. Using a walking stick, I searched among the seaweed in the deep channels and after about 50 minutes, just as the tide was turning, a sea urchin was discovered wedged in a crevice and covered with kelp. It was carefully carried some 30 metres up the shore, placed in a sheltered water-filled crevice, and left for a few minutes to settle down and extend its tube feet. The weather was bright and sunny with virtually no breeze to disturb the surface of the water. Had there been any wind, I would have searched for a sheltered spot or, in extreme conditions, abandoned the photography altogether.

Reflections of the blue sky and white clouds can cause problems but on a previous visit I had discovered, almost by chance, that a 10 x 8 in, grey, 18 per cent reflectance card which had been used to check the exposures would, if held above the specimen, cut out completely all the surface reflections. Unfortunately the shaded area did not quite fill the frame.

On this visit I had brought along a large black umbrella and, by moving it around, the surface reflections could be eliminated while the sun still shone brightly on the sea urchin. The reflection problem had been solved although passing dog-walkers must have thought me a little crazy, crouched under an umbrella on a brilliantly sunny day. (A polarising filter would absorb up to two stops and was too large a penalty to pay as I was using slow film and needed a small aperture to produce a good depth of field – and the urchin was slowly moving!)

On my way back down the shore to return the urchin, I discovered a starfish awkwardly wedged in a deep crevice. After carefully freeing it, it was placed upside down in a shallow (6 in; 15 cm) rock pool. After a minute or so, it pushed out its tube feet and very slowly began to right itself. A sequence of photographs were taken to illustrate the 'righting' process, again using the umbrella to cut out surface reflections on the water.

This is quite an easy assignment once the sea urchins and starfish have been found. The seawater in the rock pool or crevice where you are going to photograph them should be no more than 15 cm (6 in) deep to minimise distortion. Exposures of 1/30 sec or shorter are recommended as the tube feet are constantly swaying around in the water. But the biggest problem is finding the sea urchins, as they only occur on certain rocky shores right down at extreme low water (especially at spring tides); use local knowledge.

LOBSTER

The aim of this exercise (which was a chance happening) was to produce a well-composed image of a live lobster in close-up, showing details of the mouthparts, eyes and antennules.

The lobster, Homarus vulgarus, in common with other crustaceans, has a hard shell, except at the joints where it is thin and flexible to permit movement. The head/thorax is covered by a large protective shield (carapace), terminating in a sharp spear-like rostrum. There are five pairs of walking legs with pincers on the first three. The first pair bear the familiar large conspicuous claws, with the larger and stronger of the two used for cracking hard-backed food while the other slimmer claw is for grasping the food. Once caught, the food is transferred to two pairs of chewing mouthparts. The claws are also employed for attack and defence.

Although lobsters are normally found in deeper water below low tide, they often come inshore during the summer so there is always a chance of meeting this handsome blue-black creature lurking in a deep pool at low water of a spring tide.

The lobster photographs were really the result of a chance meeting. It was early September and I was on a rocky shore at a very low spring tide looking for sea urchins when I chanced upon a local fisherman collecting periwinkles. Some time later, on his way back up the shore, he proudly displayed a large lobster he had caught in a deep-water crevice, offering to let me photograph it, but not wanting to linger. I quickly squatted down and took a shot and then moved in closer, still using the 90mm macro lens. No time to set up the tripod although the overcast conditions indicated an exposure of 1/8 sec at f 5.6. Then, very quickly the T32 flash unit was attached and another exposure made before the fisherman collected his lobster and bade me farewell.

This is a straightforward exercise in the close-up photography of a live lobster, assuming you can find one. Rather than spending fruitless hours combing the shore at low water, a more productive approach would be to wait in the harbour for the return of a lobster boat and hope the skipper is amenable to your request.

This was the first hand-held shot taken some distance away and, despite the longish exposure, the image is quite sharp. Note the excellent camouflage (despite the lobster being moved onto some bare rock to make it more visible) with the very dark body blending in perfectly with the surrounding seaweed, while the sandy markings on the side of the body help to merge the lobster into the normally sandy background. Although the lighting is flat and unexciting, at least there are no black shadows obscuring the detail in the mouthpart appendages. Exposure: 1/15 sec, f 5.6. 90mm macro lens. Kodak Elite 100.

EQUIPMENT

OLYMPUS OM2n

90MM MACRO LENS

T32 FLASH UNIT

KODAK ELITE 100

The two hand-held close-ups in ambient light showed some camera shake, but the flash shot has turned out quite well. The lobster is placed at an angle in the frame, avoiding the temptation of a symmetrical, centrally positioned image which would soon become rather boring to look at. The critically important eyes are pin-sharp with an obvious eye catchlight from the flash unit, while the mouthparts, antennules, one antenna, and parts of the claws are nicely within the depth of field. The definition falls off along the body but, as the main interest is the eyes and head, this is acceptable. Exposure: flash, f 11. 90mm macro lens. Kodak Elite 100.

TIPS

❖ Be prepared to change your plans quickly if something special turns up.

❖ Grab a shot, even if conditions are not ideal i.e. poor light or witout tripod or flash unit.

❖ If time allows, select an appropriate lens, set the aperture and shutter speed and use flash if the light level is low and the subject is within three metres.

❖ With practice and experience good composition will become instinctive, needing only a few seconds to line up the subject.

WATER LOUSE

T he aim of this assignment is to photograph tiny sea creatures (e.g. water louse) using compact portable equipment, easily set up and operated on the seashore.

The water louse, Idotea baltica, is a very small creature some 15mm (3/4 in) long, yet it belongs to the same class, the Crustacea, as the lobster mentioned earlier. It therefore possesses all the crustacean features such as an external limy shell of movable plates, two pairs of antennae, mouthparts, and several pairs of legs. Idotea can be green or brown with light and dark patches along its smooth, elongated body and comes complete with two pairs of antennae and seven pairs of legs. Idotea crawls among seaweeds on the lower shore but is also a useful swimmer. A voracious feeder, it will tackle anything small which comes to hand be it animal or plant, feeding mostly at night.

Marine creatures do not travel well and are best photographed on the shore and returned to the sea afterwards. I have assembled a completely portable miniature aquarium consisting of two pieces of glass approximately 12 x 10 cm (5 x4 in) separated by a flexed length of plastic or rubber tubing and held together with two rubber bands. It was suspended from a laboratory stand which was stabilised using a piece of rock found nearby.

Lighting was provided by two flash units: one frontal and the second above and slightly behind the aquarium to provide some backlighting. The small creature, discovered on seaweed collected earlier, was placed in the tiny aquarium together with seawater and filamentous green algae.

As the magnification was greater than life-size, the 50mm macro lens was reversed to maximise the resolution and attached to the bellows unit, which was supported on a substantial tripod. Finally a piece of black card was placed behind the unit to produce a non-distracting background. Several exposures were made, after which the water louse was returned to the sea.

Although this assignment is quite tricky, calling for careful handling of the equipment and the marine creatures, it should be well within the capacity of any competent nature photographer. You should set up the outfit in a sheltered spot well up the shore (this type of work takes time and you don't want to be caught out by the tide) and once installed you could also photograph side-swimmers, aquatic spiders, the coat-of-mail chitons, and the tiny spirorbis worms in their white, chalky tubes.

A portable outfit designed to photograph small marine creatures on the seashore. The small glass cell or miniature aquarium containing the water louse was lit by two flash units linked through TTL leads to the camera. The 50mm macro lens was reversed onto an Olympus bellows unit.

The water louse foraging among the filamentous seaweed for food, which could include tiny animals or pieces of plant material. As the creature's body is parallel to the camera's film plane, everything from the head to the tail is in sharp focus with the all-important eye clearly visible. The strong backlighting has highlighted details in the translucent body, accentuated by the dark background. The three-banded water surface, with the green seaweed and the water louse reflections clearly visible, is interesting and attractive but is it too bright, thereby drawing the eye away from the Idotea. Exposure: flash, f 22, –1 stop compensation. 50mm macro lens reversed. Kodak Elite 50.

As an alternative to the method described earlier, you can use a fine-mesh net with a transparent plastic tube attached, which when trawled among the underwater seaweeds will filter the water allowing small creatures to collect in the tube.

TIPS

❖ To collect tiny marine creatures, float some wet seaweed in a tray of seawater – any creatures will soon become visible. Alternatively use the net and tube approach.

❖ When working at high magnifications, stability of equipment is vitally important – utilise rocks, large pebbles and a substantial tripod.

❖ Always use flash – powerful light source, short duration, 'freezing' any movement.

BARNACLES

Barnacles feeding is an intermittent process not readily visible to the naked eye, yet in this assignment we will try to photograph barnacles magnified up to x8, in the act of feeding, all in a well-composed picture.

Each time you walk along a rocky shore you tread on literally thousands of barnacles, probably unaware that these living animals are resting quietly until covered again by the rising tide. The common, or rock, barnacle, Balanus balanoides, was aptly described by Louis Agassiz as 'nothing more than a little shrimplike animal, lying on its back in a limestone house and kicking food into its mouth'. To photograph barnacles magnified up to 8x requires working precision not possible on the seashore. I had to collect the barnacles. The easiest way is not to try to remove them from the rocks but to find a few barnacle-covered limpets. Give the limpet a sharp tap and it will usually release itself from the rock surface. Several were collected with some seawater, taken home and kept in a domestic fridge (9ºC, 48ºF – about the same temperature as the sea). Every twelve hours or so I alternately exposed and submerged the barnacles by tilting the container to simulate tidal action.

The barnacle-covered limpets were carefully placed in a small home-made aquarium, measuring 30 x 20 x 7 cm, and allowed to settle down. Within minutes the hatches slowly opened and the barnacles started feeding – so far so good!

The camera, bellows unit and the 80mm macro lens were assembled using the powerful Metz 45 as a backlight (hoping to highlight the delicate feeding legs) and a small piece of white card to reflect some light onto the front surfaces of the barnacles.

EQUIPMENT

OLYMPUS OM2N
20MM AND 80MM MACRO LENSES,
BELLOWS UNIT,
METZ 45 CT4 AND OLYMPUS T20
FLASH UNITS,
SMALL AQUARIUM,
BENBO TRIPOD,
HAND-HELD SPOTLIGHT.

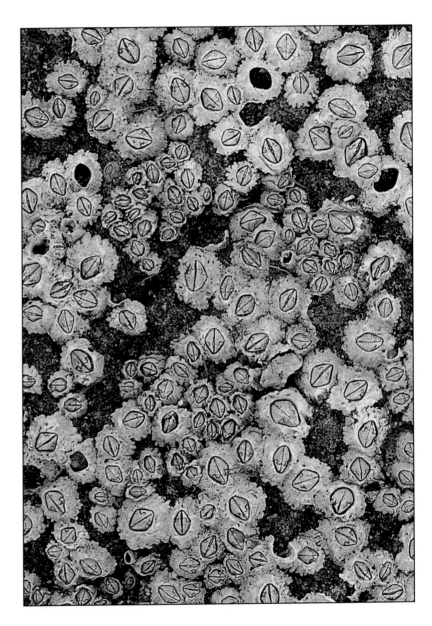

The tide is out, the hatches are battened down as the barnacles rest, waiting for the next tide. The shells with black holes in the top are dead and empty; the rest are all alive. Exposure: 1/30 sec, f 11. Provia 100. Yorkshire Coast, England.

Above: Taken with the 80 mm macro lens, this shows the barnacles growing almost on top of each other in the struggle for space. The anterior surfaces of the barnacles are rather underlit despite using a white reflector close to the front of the tank. Depth of field could not be increased as the lens was set at its minimum aperture. Exposure: flash, f 22, −1 stop compensation. Velvia 50.

Right: A small T32 flash unit provided some frontal lighting, while the powerful Metz 45 was again used as a backlight, nicely highlighting the delicately fringed legs. Caught at the peak of the action, the legs are just on the point of quickly redrawing into the shell. The depth of field of less than 1mm did not allow complete sharpness across the arched legs but as the 20mm macro lens was stopped down to its minimum aperture there was little I could do about it. To the left another barnacle is just beginning its feeding cycle as the curved legs start to emerge. Exposure: flash, f 16, −1 stop compensation. Velvia 50.

Although the 80mm lens is only a lens head, it does have some built-in fine focusing plus an automatic diaphragm, making it fairly easy to use with an automatic bellows unit. However the 20mm macro lens has no built-in focusing and only a manual diaphragm resulting in severe focusing problems due to the slight backlash in the rack-and-pinion mechanism of the bellows unit – sufficient to throw the image well out of focus.

Using the lens stopped down to its minimum aperture of f16 on a longish bellows extension resulted in the viewfinder image being almost too dark to even see. I decided to use a powerful hand-held spotlight and with practice developed the following sequence: switch on the spotlight, focus on the barnacle's waving legs, switch off the light and release the shutter and flash units just prior to the very quick withdrawal of the legs. Practice makes perfect but almost a roll of film was used before I got everything synchronised.

This is an advanced piece of work requiring lots of time and infinite patience. However if you are prepared to build a small aquarium

(glass, not plastic) and can obtain the necessary barnacle-encrusted limpets, then you should certainly have a go at it. Use your standard (or macro) lens in the reverse position as the image will be larger than life-size and the lens will produce sharper images. Alternatively a high quality 50mm enlarging lens reversed onto the bellows unit will deliver quite excellent results but without built-in focusing or an automatic diaphragm the lens will be slightly more awkward to use.

TIPS

❖ Working at magnifications of up to 8 x life-size requires accurately set-up and firmly anchored equipment.

❖ Lots of patience and time needed – can't rush this type of work.

❖ Bracket exposure quite widely – be prepared to use plenty of film as success rates are low.

SEA CLIFFS AND ROCKY ISLANDS

If birds of the open sea could breed on water, they would never come on land at all. As they have no choice, their stay is as short as possible, commensurate with laying their eggs and feeding the young, but once the breeding season is over they head out to sea again, never to return until next spring.

As their breeding grounds seem to be limited, with very difficult access (for humans and animals), once a successful site has been established, the colonies tend to grow rapidly with thousands of birds crowded onto rocks, ledges, cliff tops and stacks.

Britain has about 70 per cent of the world's population of razorbills, which breed around our coasts but spend the rest of the year in the North Sea and North Atlantic. Similarly Britain also supports more than 70 per cent of the world's gannets with very large colonies on the gigantic stacks on St Kilda and on Bass Rock in the Firth of Forth. The sole mainland breeding colony of gannets in Britain is on the 400ft (120m) high cliffs at Bempton in Yorkshire. At the end of the breeding season, they migrate out into the North Sea and Atlantic, with the youngest going as far south as the West African coast.

To visit a seabird colony during the breeding season is to walk into a cacophony of sound, the volume of which almost beggars belief, while the stench of guano can be quite overpowering at times. But by late August the sea cliffs become eerily silent as the birds return to the open sea and the whole cycle begins again.

Large colonies of grey seals can be seen in the sea around the Farne Islands. The photograph was taken from a boat on the journey out to the seabird colonies. Exposure: 1/125 sec, f 8. Kodak Elite 200.

The offshore stacks of the Pinnacles near
Staple Island, one of the outer islands
in the Farne group. The fissures and
scrapes in the rocks were left as the last
Ice Age retreated some 10,000 years ago
and today all the usable surfaces are
occupied by thousands of guillemots.
Also present are kittiwakes, identified
by their straggly nests; plus a few shags.
The photograph was taken from the boat
going out to the Farne Islands. Exposure:
1/250 sec, f 8. 75–300mm lens.
Fuji Sensia 100.

KITTIWAKE

The purpose of this assignment is to portray kittiwakes, preferably with their young, in a typical cliff-top nest, at the height of the breeding season.

The kittiwake, Rissa tridactyla, has remained faithful to the sea, spending much of the year over the oceans feeding on fish, surface invertebrates and the leftovers from fishing vessels. Because it spends so little time on land its legs are relatively short, lacking the hind toe or hallux; hence its species name of tridactyla – three toes. Kittiwakes nest mainly on ledges on cliff faces, building cup-shaped nests consisting of dry seaweeds and other local materials such as pieces of fishing net, cemented together and to the cliff ledge with liberal amounts of guano. The eggs (one to three), which are grey to buff-brown with dark blotches and spots, are laid in May and June and hatch after 28 days with the young leaving the nest some 40 - 45 days later.

The common name 'kittiwake' derives from the cries of 'kit-ee-wayke' which fill the air during the breeding season, but by early September the nesting grounds become silent as all the cliff-nesting birds return to the open sea.

The photographs were taken on the Farne Islands a few miles off the Northumberland coast. Access to the Inner and Outer Farnes is by boat with frequent trips from nearby Seahouses. My visit was towards the end of June when most of the seabirds were either incubating their eggs or feeding the young. When we arrived on the Inner Farne it was early afternoon with the overhead sun shining from a clear blue sky. The weather on the north east coast is often cold and windy with visits to the islands being dependent on favourable sea conditions.

Because of the well-earned popularity of the Farne Islands during the breeding season, visitors are restricted to well-marked paths and viewing points, so you follow the route taking photographs as they arise.

I set up the camera and tripod at one of the cliff-top viewing points and selected the 75 - 300 telephoto, setting it at around 200mm. Several shots were taken from slightly different positions using vertical and horizontal formats. Because exposures were often in the region of 1/60 second or longer at f 11, the precise moment for releasing the shutter was critical if blurred heads and beaks were to be avoided.

This is an easy assignment for a competent nature photographer equipped with a good tripod and a medium-length zoom lens. As your time on the island is very limited, you should concentrate on one or two sites per visit rather than attempt to cover the whole island each time. The high cliffs and the almost inevitable north-easterly wind provide a good opportunity for some seabirds-in-flight photography (see later assignment).

EQUIPMENT

OLYMPUS OM2N

SIGMA 75–300MM ZOOM

SIGMA 500MM

MINOLTA 7000I

AUTOFOCUS CAMERA

70–210MM ZOOM

KODAK ELITE 100 AND 400 FILM.

TIPS

❖ Best conditions for photographing contrasty black and white seabirds are bright sun with very thin cloud cover.

❖ As daylight only is being used, the camera should be very firmly mounted as longish exposures (1/30 sec) and long lenses (300–500 mm) can result in subject blur and/or camera shake.

❖ Use a UV or skylight filter to protect lens from salt in the atmosphere.

The overall composition is satisfactory, with the nest forming a solid base to the picture while the vertical cliff face to the right helps to form the frame. Fortunately the white guano on the nest is in shadow cast by the parent bird and therefore not too prominent while the very dark background is ideal as it helps to highlight the bird. The latter is parallel to the camera film plane and is therefore in sharp focus from its beak to its tail. The beak is open and the all-important eye, although in light shadow, is well defined. The two youngsters, nicely protected by the mother, are looking straight at the camera with both beaks open and all four eyes clearly visible. The fine, fluffy down feathers are pleasantly highlighted against the dark background of the mother's wing feathers. However the overhead lighting is slightly too contrasty, resulting in some slight loss of detail on the kittiwake's head and tail, while the white cliff face is too light in tone and a little distracting.

Exposure: 1/60 sec, f 11. 75–300mm zoom. Kodak Elite 100. Farne Islands, Northumberland.

ARCTIC TERN

T he aim of this exercise is to photograph an Arctic tern in flight and with its young during the short three or so weeks when the chicks are still around the nest.

The Arctic tern, Sterna paradisaea, spends several months of the year in the Antarctic where the food-rich waters allow it to build up its energy store ready for the very long flight north. It breeds around the shores of the Arctic Ocean, North Atlantic and Pacific. On average, an Arctic tern covers some 20,000 miles each year on its migration flights and, as it can live for up to 25 years, this could add up to the equivalent of a return trip to the moon!

Arctic tern hovers in the air prior to landing in the nesting area, with the tail feathers spread out to act as an air brake. Exposure: 1/500 sec, f8. 75–300mm lens. Kodak Elite 400.

EQUIPMENT

OLYMPUS OM2n

75–300MM ZOOM

KODAK ELITE 100

This Arctic tern with its chick was taken towards the end of the afternoon with the sun quite low in the sky. The placing of the parent bird is satisfactory with everything in sharp focus, while the backlighting nicely highlights the texture and detail in the feathers. The young chick, although partially masked by the green leaf in front of it, is also attractively lit as the low sun just grazes the top of its head. Unfortunately the black eye of the parent (without a catchlight) set in a black head makes it almost invisible. But whether the chick looking in the opposite direction to the parent adds interest to the picture or merely confuses things, I'm not quite sure. Exposure: 1/30 sec, f 11. 75–300mm zoom. Kodak Elite 100.

Colonies, containing several thousand birds, are found on shingle beaches, short turf and rocky islands, with their nests being little more than a scraping in the ground, often lined with a few tufts of grass, small twigs and pieces of broken shell. Two or three buff eggs with heavy brown markings are laid in mid-May to June and hatch after about 23 days. The fledglings fly three to four weeks later.

The photographs were taken on the Inner Farne Island off the Northumberland coast (see previous assignment). These islands represent the overlap zone between the common tern and the Arctic tern, which can be distinguished by the former having a red beak with a black tip, and shorter tail streamers, while the latter has a pure red beak and long tail streamers. However on the Inner Farne there are Arctic terns with orange beaks, some with black tips and some without. Their identification was confirmed by one of the ornithologists living on the islands.

Entering a tern colony during the breeding season can be a very unnerving experience for first-timers as the birds swoop down and strike the birdwatchers' heads, which is why protective headgear is recommended. We discovered that holding an extended tripod aloft like a folded umbrella prevented the birds from striking.

The method used was quite straightforward, involving carrying the tripod-mounted camera up the path and setting it up near a tern on the nest or with its young. The telephoto lens was usually set near the 200mm mark, with exposures in the region of 1/30 to 1/60 sec at apertures from f 11 to f 16 depending on the ambient conditions.

This is a fairly straightforward assignment as the terns' nests are at ground level and easy to locate. Some will still be incubating their eggs and you should look for a low viewpoint where at least part of an egg is visible (which is not so easy). When photographing the parent and chicks, wait until the wandering young return to the parent as this will result in a more compact family grouping. Try photographing terns in flight using ISO 200-400 film, allowing around 1/500 sec exposure.

TIPS

❖ **Wear protective headgear, as terns will mob you on entering the colony.**

❖ **Use medium telephoto lens to distance you from the bird and prevent any anxiety.**

❖ **Taking photographs is not a problem – bird just sits on the eggs waiting to be snapped. Low viewpoint is more natural and intimate than shooting from the standing position.**

PUFFIN

The purpose of this assignment is to produce a portfolio of puffin images including standing close-ups and in-flight shots.

The puffin, Fratercula arctica, is probably the best known of all seabirds, with its comical appearance and Charlie Chaplin walk being familiar to everyone, yet many people have never seen a live puffin. The most striking feature, the large multicoloured beak, is used as a digging tool, for fighting and courtship, and as a wonderful collector and transporter of sand eels, whiting, and sprats. It manages to carry up to a dozen or so in a neatly arranged row by 'dislocating' its beak at the hinge end, permitting the upper and lower halves to close parallel to each other. This allows all the fish to be gripped equally firmly along the whole length of the beak rather than just in the narrow angle at the inner end.

The puffin, which belongs to the auk family (razorbill, guillemot, little auk) has a stout, heavy body relative to its wing size and as a result has a high stalling speed. It almost has to throw itself off the cliff edge to pick up sufficient speed to fly and, when taking off from the surface of the sea, it uses its webbed feet to run through the water, with the wings beating furiously. The wings are just as useful in the sea as in the air, where they are used for propulsion, giving the impression that the puffin is 'flying' underwater.

The photographs were taken on the Farne Islands at the same time as the kittiwake and Arctic tern shots. For static images I used a 75–300mm zoom and a 500mm lens with the camera firmly mounted on a tripod and the shutter tripped using a cable release. In-flight shots were taken with a 70–210mm auto-focus lens; the camera was hand-held but stabilised on a monopod.

This not too difficult assignment does require sharp reflexes and the ability to pan quickly and accurately. A good range of telephoto lenses is necessary and for static shots you should use a substantial tripod – for in-flight work a monopod is the best solution. Very short (1/500 sec or less) exposures and fast film are necessary because puffins beat their short wings very rapidly and never glide.

A puffin working very hard to become air-borne, as it 'runs' through the water with its wings beating furiously to pick up speed and gain some lift. The shot was taken hastily from the boat crossing to the Farnes and, due to the speed of the action, manual focusing, and the inappropriately slow (ISO 100) film, the image could be sharper, but it does, at least, suggest dynamic action.
Exposure: 1/125 sec, ƒ5.6. 75–300mm lens. Kodak Elite 100.

A puffin with beak full of sand eels returning at great speed to feed its young. A heavy body and short stubby wings requires vigorous flapping to stay airborne, with the high shutter speed unable to 'freeze' the wing tips. Exposure: 1/000 sec, ƒ5.6. 300mm lens. Fuji Sensia 400.

This puffin has just left its burrow and is heading out to sea in search of sand eels. The undercarriage (webbed feet) has already been raised to streamline the body and reduce drag. A panning movement helped to hold the puffin in frame, while the short exposure kept the wings fairly sharply defined. Exposure: 1/1000 sec, f 5.6, 300mm lens. Fuji Sensia 400.

TIPS

❖ Go equipped with lens range 300–500 mm and a substantial tripod.

❖ For in-flight shots, use fast film (ISO 200–400) and a fast lens – puffins are typical auks with a fast wing-beat.

The two puffins gazing out to sea are positioned in the frame to give them plenty of space to look into (or jump into!). Both are pin-sharp with the soft diffused daylight from a lightly overcast sky bringing out the delicate detail in the white breast feathers and in the areas below the eyes. A solid slab of rock forms a good base to the picture while the nearby cliff background is well out of focus – one of the few advantages of using a 500mm lens is the shallow depth of field. Exposure: 1/60 sec, f 8. 500mm lens. Fuji Sensia 100.

GANNET IN FLIGHT

The aim of this exercise is to produce well-composed images of gannets in flight.

The gannet, Sula bassana, is a huge seabird with a wingspan of almost 2 metres and an appetite to match. When not breeding it spends its time at sea gently gliding on the wind, ever watchful of the food supply swimming in the sea below. A long, sharp, dagger-shaped beak and forward-pointing eyes give good binocular vision, and on seeing a fish, the gannet pulls back its wings into the high-speed diving configuration and rockets down from as high as 100 ft into the sea and onto the unsuspecting fish. The gannet returns each year to its nesting colony on the top of sea stacks and cliff ledges and from March to September the air is alive with the screeching roar of gannets. Two-thirds of the world's gannet population is to be found in the 13 gannetries around the British Isles of which only one, at Bempton Cliffs in Yorkshire, is a mainland colony, the rest being on offshore islands. Very large colonies are to be found on the Bass Rock in the Firth of Forth and St Kilda in the Outer Hebrides. Gannets take five years to reach maturity with the youngest migrating furthest, reaching West African waters in their first year. Sub-adults (3 - 4 years old) winter in the Mediterranean and Biscay, while mature adults stay in the home waters of the North Sea and East Atlantic outside the breeding season.

This shot shows a young adult about to land on its nest. The gannet is well positioned in the frame with the all-important head and beak sharply defined.

As the bird is approaching the nest, the legs and large webbed feet, normally tucked up under the abdomen, have been lowered not only for landing but also to act as an air brake to reduce the speed. The tail feathers are spread out and held almost vertically to decrease the speed before landing. Due to the low speed, the normally smooth airflow over the trailing edge of the wings has broken down, slightly ruffling the feathers; the gannet is about to stall. The overcast conditions have resulted in lower contrast, recording detail in the white, light-reflecting feathers of the gannet. Exposure: 1/500 sec, f 8. 400 mm Tokina AT-X lens. Kodak Elite 400. Bempton Cliffs gannetry, North Yorkshire.

EQUIPMENT

MINOLTA 7000I
AUTOFOCUS SLR CAMERA
TOKINA AT-X 400MM
F5.6 AUTOFOCUS LENS
SIGMA 1.4X TELECONVERTER
MONOPOD.

A gannet in typical gliding flight with the wings fully outstretched, using the off-sea breeze rising up the cliff face. It is well positioned in the frame with the diagonal image suggesting dynamic action, although in gliding flight the gannet is using the minimum of effort and therefore very little energy. Flying directly towards the camera always looks impressive, particularly when the head, beak and eyes are in sharp focus. Being critical, the head-on position of the gannet does not show any details of wing- or body-shape, with the bird image occupying less than 10 per cent of the frame area. The lens was focused manually. Exposure: 1/500 sec, f 8. 400mm lens. 1.4x converter. Kodak Elite 400.

I visited the Bempton Cliffs gannetry on several occasions during the summer months in weather which varied from cloudless and sunny to bright but completely overcast. As the gannet is white with black wingtips, it did not photograph well on cloudless days due to the high contrast lighting, which usually resulted in lack of detail in the white feathers. Bright overcast days were much better.

Fast ISO 400 slide film was used (set at 600 to ensure good colour saturation) with the 400mm lens plus occasionally the 1.4x converter.

The Minolta was hand-held but supported on a slightly tightened ball-and-socket head screwed onto a substantial monopod. This allowed sufficient movement to follow the flight of a gannet while at the same time reducing possible camera shake. Exposures of 1/500 second (or occasionally 1/250 when light level was low) were used on shutter priority. The autofocus mechanism did not work well with the rather bland grey/white of the gannet's feathers and would not function at all with the 1.4x converter in place. For around half of the shots I focused the lens manually.

This is quite a difficult assignment if your aim is to produce acceptably large, well-defined images of gannets in flight. Practise panning shots and remember to follow through after the shutter has been released. Birds flying directly towards you require either a pre-focused camera or a very efficient autofocus system, although the latter often has difficulty coping with the unbroken white of the gannet's body.

TIPS

❖ Wear plenty of warm clothing – cliff tops are very exposed places.

❖ Use a short exposure of 1/500 sec if possible – helps to 'freeze' the bird's wings but also reduces the possibility of camera shake when using a longish (e.g. 400mm) lens.

❖ Study the flight path of one or two birds and, if possible, position yourself parallel to it, swinging the camera while keeping the bird in the centre of the viewfinder.

CHAPTER SIX

Woodlands

As the last Ice Age retreated some 15,000 years ago, woodland began to replace the stunted tundra vegetation of mosses, lichens and dwarf plants which covered much of the land. The first woodlands were mainly birch with some willow and aspen but, as the climate became warmer, Scots pine took over as the dominant tree. Over a long period of time and as the temperatures kept on rising it was replaced from the south by broad-leaved trees such as elm, oak, beech and alder until eventually much of Britain was covered with deciduous forests. The original pines were limited to northern Scotland where they still survive today.

About 5,000 years ago primitive man began to clear extensive areas of forest for pasture, cultivation, fuel and building materials and by the Norman Conquest many large areas of woodland had already gone. As the insatiable appetite for timber continued, the remaining woodland was further reduced until today less than 8 per cent of Britain is wooded, much of it either 'managed' or 'new' coniferous forests. Norway spruce and European larch were introduced some 200 years ago, mainly by wealthy landowners as ornamental trees, but the really extensive planting of conifers for commercial profit began after the Forestry Commission was formed in 1919.

Broad-leaved woodland in full autumn colours. As the tree roots have difficulty taking in water from the frozen ground, the leaves, which are always giving off water, must be shed. The breaking down of the leaf pigments resulting in the attractive autumn colours is an important part of the leaf-fall process. Exposure: 1/15 sec, f16, 90mm lens, Fuji Provia 100.

On examining the original transparency it was obvious that the foreground mixture of scattered bluebells among emerging bracken and brambles added little to the overall image. The lower section was cropped to produce a panoramic format which concentrates the eye on the horizontal sweep of densely packed bluebells. The top and sides are well framed with sycamores, which on the right side are, unfortunately, a little too well lit and therefore slightly distracting.
Exposure: 1/15 sec, f 16. 90mm lens. Fuji Provia 100.

Huge swaths of higher ground are now covered with dense pine and spruce forests, which support a very poor wildlife population. Many coniferous forests now have broad-leaved inserts at various points, which help to encourage wildlife and restore the balance of nature.Broad-leaved woodland, on the other hand, includes the most diverse range of plants and animals in any habitat outside the tropics, all interdependent and governed by well-marked seasonal changes. During the winter plants are dormant and animal life is scarce, yet at ground level micro-fungi and tiny invertebrates are breaking down the carpet of dead leaves and plants, returning the nutrients to the soil. In spring with the onset of warmer weather and a plentiful supply of rain, trees and flowering plants spring into life again, providing sap, pollen and nectar for the burgeoning insect population. Animals and birds become very active as the breeding season gets underway. During the summer woodland trees are in full leaf and growth continues at a pace, with warmth, light, water and food readily available for the plant and animal populations. With the approach of autumn everything slows down again as many animals either hibernate or die, while shrubs and trees, unable to extract water from the frozen ground, shed their leaves which are giving off large amounts of water the plant can ill afford to lose.

In this chapter I will be discussing a range of photographic assignments based on selected trees (sweet chestnut, pine, maple, larch), fungi (fly agaric, puff-ball), and mammals (red squirrel, deer, badger), all of which are natural residents of woodlands. Woodland birds such as the long-tailed tit, great spotted woodpecker, sparrowhawk and jay also frequent many gardens and they have been included in the appropriate section in the chapter on urban gardens.

BLUEBELL WOOD IN SPRING

Location Workshop

T he aim of this assignment is to try to capture the feelings engendered when strolling through a woodland scene surrounded by carpets of bluebells in full bloom.

The common bluebell, Endymion non-scriptus, belongs to the family Liliaceae which are perennial herbs with underground rhizomes or bulbs and sheathing lanceolate leaves. Bluebell bulbs survive the winter underground and as the temperature rises in the early spring, the first leaves begin to appear and make food before the overhead leaf canopy of the broad-leaved trees develop and shut out the sunlight.

Most of my time was spent walking through woods looking for a suitable viewpoint and, as so often happens, the breathtaking sight of carpets of lightly-scented bluebells does not look quite so exciting when studied in two dimensions through the camera viewfinder.

One or two shots were taken of carpets of bluebells among the trees and then I concentrated on woodland paths and good composition. The colour of bluebells is quite difficult to capture accurately on film because the flowers reflect quite a lot of red and infrared light converting themselves into 'mauve bells'. Each shot was duplicated using a pale blue 82B filter (which I later discovered was too strong).

The early afternoon May sun was quite high in the sky with patches of thin cloud around. Exposures were made when the sun was lightly veiled in cloud to reduce the very contrasty lighting. Exposures were usually either 1/8 or 1/15 second at f 22 using both reflected (off a Kodak grey card) and incident light readings. As usual the camera was firmly mounted on the Benbo tripod and the shutter tripped using a cable release.

This is a straightforward exercise, but many well-known bluebell woods are being over-walked to the detriment of the plants. Look hard for unknown, off the beaten track examples. Check the emergence of the flowers on a twice-weekly basis (if convenient), taking your photographs when most of the flowers are at their best (they develop and open from the bottom of the stem upwards).

Bluebells and red campions growing together at the base of a sycamore which is providing a satisfactorily dark background for the flowers.
Exposure: 1/30 sec, f 8. Mamiya 6. Fuji Provia 100.

EQUIPMENT

FUJI GW 670 RANGEFINDER CAMERA

FIXED 90MM F3.5 FUJINON LENS

FUJI SENSIA FILM (ISO 100)

BENBO TRIPOD

CABLE RELEASE

SELECTION OF FILTERS.

This would seem to sum up what you could hope for in a picture entitled 'Walk through a bluebell wood'. There are bluebells in abundance with the camera height adjusted to show the greatest numbers of flowers while at the same time including some trees in the upper quarter of the frame. The narrow path leads the eye from the left foreground up and across the picture through an area of maximum concentration of flowers. The dappled hazy sunshine adds atmosphere to the scene while the sycamores at the sides and top plus the dark foreground all help to frame the picture and concentrate the eye on the masses of bluebells. Exposure: 1/8 sec, f22. Standard 90mm lens. Fuji Provia 100.

TIPS

❖ Steer clear of cloudless, sunny days – too much contrast in a bluebell wood.

❖ Choose a still, windless day as swaying bluebell flowers look natural but will be blurred in the picture.

❖ As the woodland scenes usually have depth with plenty of foreground, use a tripod and stop the lens right down to obtain the maximum depth of field.

❖ Modern films record bluebells pretty well – but by all means use a pale blue 82A filter for some of the shots.

FLOWERS OF THE LARCH

The newly formed crimson flowers of the larch are fairly inconspicuous and easily overlooked and in this assignment we hope to produce close-up images to show the delicate beauty of their structure.

The larch, Larix decidua, as the name suggests is alone among our conifers in being a deciduous tree. In the winter it is bare and skeletal; in the spring and summer it displays its bright green livery and as autumn approaches the green needles turn a rich brown before falling to the ground.

The deep crimson female flowers, some 20mm (0.8 in) long, are usually found on two-year-old needle-bearing shoots. Each flower consists of spirally arranged surface scales and small yellowish seed scales containing two ovules per scale.

The male flowers are small and inconspicuous but they produce the pollen necessary to fertilise the female flowers. After fertilisation the ovules develop into winged seeds, which are shed from September until the following spring and after about five years the old cones, and the dried out branches to which they are attached, drop from the tree – a good example of natural pruning.

Thinking about the composition of the final picture, one or two twigs each containing at least two flowers in close proximity were collected and taken home.

Working outdoors, but wanting to have some control over the lighting, I decided to use low level daylight, supplemented by the artificial illumination from two small video lights. They were effective when held 7–8 cm from the flowers and when covered with a piece of pale blue acetate sheet (to raise the colour temperature nearer to daylight), the effect was quite pleasing. After some experimenting the video lights were held on either side of flowers, slightly behind them and tilted down at around 45º with the low level daylight providing the basic all round lighting.

The 80mm macro lens was set at f 16–22, approximately focused using the adjustable auto-tube and accurately focused using the fine focusing built into the lens head. A green/brown background board was placed about 1 metre (39 in) behind the flowers and lit by ambient daylight.

Composition and lighting are all important in this shot. The twig is tilted up slightly which is more attractive than a purely horizontal placement. The two crimson flowers are sufficiently close together to avoid leaving a yawning gap in the centre of the frame, but far enough apart to occupy the visually strong points ('rule of thirds'). The hand-held video lights almost backlight the flowers, lifting them nicely from the dark green out-of-focus background. On the negative side, the cluster of green needles on the left is too close to the flower and a little distracting. Exposure: 2 sec, f 22, –2/3 stop compensation. 80mm macro lens. Fuji Velvia.

EQUIPMENT

OLYMPUS OM2n

80MM MACRO LENS

TELESCOPIC AUTO TUBE

TWO SMALL 40 WATT
HAND-HELD VIDEO LIGHTS

TRIPOD

VELVIA FILM

Due to my forgetfulness the twigs were left outdoors. Overnight rain resulted in large beads of water collecting on the flowers and leaves. I used ambient daylight supplemented by frontal and semi backlight video lighting and am particularly pleased with the crystalline quality of the water droplets highlighted against the dark background. Exposure: 2 sec, f 22, –2/3 stop compensation. 80mm macro lens. Fuji Velvia.

TIPS

❖ Mixing daylight and artificial light can cause unattractive colour biases. Try different strengths of blue filtration on the artificial light source.

❖ When working at life-size magnification, the camera must be firmly mounted on a tripod to avoid camera shake.

❖ As the depth of field is very shallow in close-up work, a small lens aperture (f22) is advisable.

MOUNTAIN PINE

The aim of this assignment is to photograph mountain pine male flowers liberating clouds of pollen.

There are quite a few large shrubby mountain pine locally and in early June I began checking the pollen levels by gently tapping one or two branches. When pollen production seemed to be reaching its peak, three small branches were very carefully removed and transported home in a plastic box (better than a plastic bag – no squashing).

They were then taken up into the studio (converted loft), stood in water and left for a day or two to fully ripen. You are rather working in the dark because if you tap a branch too vigorously you may well lose most of the pollen before even making the first exposure.

Flash lighting, used to 'freeze' the moving twig and the pollen cloud, was positioned behind the branch to backlight the pollen. Two flash units were set up (one at either side), about 45° behind and 45° above the supported pine branch, each with a taped-on piece of card to prevent the flash light spilling into the camera lens. The tripod-mounted camera was linked to the flash units through TTL leads and the shutter was tripped using a cable release.

The technique was to tap the branch with a pencil and almost simultaneously fire the shutter and flash units. Unfortunately it was all too easy to include the pencil in the photograph, to tap the branch so forcefully as to move it partially out of frame and out of focus, or to tap it too gently resulting in beautifully framed and focused branch but no pollen in sight.

The set-up was varied slightly by changing the black velvet background for a dark mottled green one, while for some of the shots I placed a white board in front of the branch to reflect a little light onto the male flower cluster. Thirty exposures were made during a three-hour session by which time all the pollen had been shed from the three sets of male flowers.

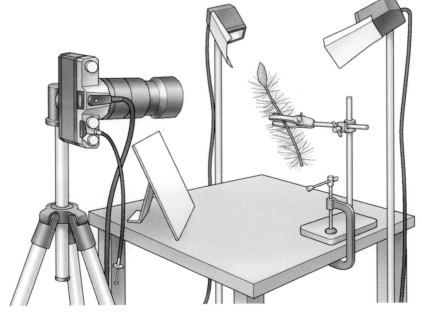

The set-up showing the clamped branch with two flash units providing powerful backlighting, and a white card reflecting a little light onto the front surfaces. Note the TTL flash leads and the long cable release hanging down from the camera.

EQUIPMENT

OLYMPUS OM2n

90MM TAMRON MACRO LENS

2 x T32 FLASH UNITS

TRIPOD

BACKGROUND BOARDS,

KODAK EKTACHROME 64.

Above: Despite tapping the branch quite vigorously, the male flowers and all the surrounding needles are well placed in the frame and pin-sharp. You can imagine a wind blowing from the right side, bending the branch and dispersing the pollen to the left where it meets the eye viewing the picture from the left side. The black background is obviously non-distracting but I'm not sure whether it helps to give the picture depth. Another criticism might be that the upper male flower cluster is almost devoid of pollen due to too long a time lag between tapping and exposing, allowing the pollen to completely clear the upper flower cluster.
Exposure: flash, f 16, 1 stop underexposure. 2 x T32 flash units. 90mm macro lens. Kodak Ektachrome 64.

Above right: This shot includes the dark green background which in many ways I prefer to the black one. Despite a quite vigorous tapping of the branch, the male flowers and the surrounding needles are all nicely framed and quite sharp. The branch is leaning to the left suggesting dynamic activity with the area around the flowers filled with a well-defined pollen cloud. The dark green background looks more natural (but less dramatic) than the black one, with its dark colours harmonising well with the green needles and brown twig. Exposure: flash, f 16, 1 stop underexposure. 2 x T32 flash units. 90mm macro lens. Kodak Ektachrome 64.

TIPS

❖ Always look for complete, undamaged specimens.

❖ Black backgrounds require –2/3 to –1 2/3 stops underexposure. Extensive bracketing is the only way to guarantee a 'correctly' exposed transparency.

❖ As it is very difficult to predict exactly how an object lit solely by flash will turn out, check the set-up by using a hand-held video light in the same position.

THE FLY AGARIC FUNGUS

T he purpose of this assignment is to photograph the fly agaric in its natural environment, showing if possible, different stages in its development.

The fly agaric, Amanita muscaria, is a well known, very conspicuous fungus identified by its bright cap (pileus) covered with small white patches of soft, felt-like tissue. It is widely distributed in pine woods and under birch trees. The fly agaric is a favourite subject for artists and craftsmen and one of the few fungi featured widely in children's books; unfortunately it and its relatives, the Death Cap and the Panther Cap, are extremely poisonous. An infusion of the cap in milk was once used to kill flies – hence its name.

The fungi were found in local woodland under birch trees during late October. The photographs were taken mid-afternoon. I visit this woodland most days when walking the dog and over the years have discovered three or four sites where fly agarics appear each autumn. Finding perfect specimens is difficult because children often damage them, while slugs and snails soon eat holes in the caps.The specimens were growing on a low bank under a bracken frond, but they were covered with pieces of grass, twigs and dead leaves. I spent some time spraying water on the caps and stalks using a small plant sprayer, before carefully removing the offending material with a small paintbrush.

The tripod-mounted camera was set very low to view the fungi from ground level, allowing the annulus to be seen under the well-developed cap. As the weather was overcast with no direct sunlight, a small hand-held video light with a pale blue filter over the lens provided a highlight and some modelling. To throw the background out of focus a modest lens aperture of f 8 was used, as a larger aperture would not have produced sufficient depth of field to keep both the stalks and the near edges of the caps in sharp focus. The exposure was 1/15 second, using a cable release to trip the shutter. Both horizontal and vertical formats were used and on several frames blurred movement of the bracken was produced by blowing on the bracken frond.

This is an easy assignment once you have found some attractive undamaged specimens. Fungi photographed at ground level result in a more 'intimate' image than when photographed from above. Almost any focal length macro lens can be used.

EQUIPMENT

BRONICA ETRSi MEDIUM
FORMAT SLR CAMERA

100MM MACRO LENS

TRIPOD

SMALL VIDEO LIGHT

PLANT SPRAYER
AND SMALL PAINTBRUSH,

FUJI PROVIA 100 FILM.

Fly agarics in the snow – a rare occurrence. It was late November and we had a very early fall of snow but by the time I arrived in the wood, the wet snow was melting quickly. Two strokes of luck – the early snow, and the fungi still in excellent condition so late in their season.
Exposure: 1/60 sec, f 11. 90mm macro lens. Kodak Elite 100.

Various stages in the development of the fly agaric are illustrated, with the red caps being a prominent feature. Side lighting provided by the video light has been effective as shots taken without it looked quite flat. The f 8 aperture kept the four fungi and the surrounding area quite sharp while allowing the background to go well out of focus. I was quite pleased with the green background as red and green complement each other, with red always being to the fore. The image was selected to point up the contrast between the swaying bracken and the completely static nature of the fungi.

The picture could have been improved by using an even lower viewpoint to show the gills under the fungal caps, while a slightly sloping foreground would have made a more interesting composition. Exposure: 1/15 sec, f 8. Bronica ETRSi 100mm macro lens. Fuji Provia 100.

TIPS

❖ As all 'toadstools' grow at ground level, using a right angle finder attached to the camera eyepiece is much better than lying prone on wet grass.

❖ Damaged, misshapen fungi occur naturally but look quite unsightly on the finished photograph – avoid them.

❖ Many fungi caps are covered with pieces of grass, plant roots and general debris – gently remove it using a plant mist sprayer and a paintbrush.

❖ If the natural light is flat and dull, using a small hand-held video light will add a little modelling and sparkle to the image.

PUFF-BALL DISPERSING SPORES

T he purpose of this indoor workshop is to produce a well-composed image of a ripe puff-ball dispersing a cloud of spores.

The common puff-ball, Lycoperdon periatum, is an inverted pear shaped fungus up to 75 mm (3 in) tall and 50 mm (2 in) across, growing in pastures or grassy areas in woods and woodland verges. It lacks chlorophyll and, being unable to make its own food, it obtains its nourishment by feeding on the decaying remains of dead animals and plants (saprophytic).

The puff-balls were discovered on the edge of a local wood one morning in early November. A cluster of three plus the surrounding earth and leaf litter was carefully dug up and transported home in a shallow tray.It was arranged with the more powerful T32 flash unit placed 30 cm (12 in) above and slightly behind the puff-balls (backlighting), with the less powerful T20 unit positioned at subject level 60 cm (24 in) to the right and slightly in front. I then placed the background board some 60 cm behind the puff-balls.

Several shots were taken, after which the T20 flash unit was moved just behind the puff-balls, using a white reflector to lighten their frontal surfaces.

Spore dispersal can be initiated by tapping the puff-ball with a pencil or by setting up a mechanical 'tapper' behind the specimens. I opted for the latter, using an off-the-shelf pneumatic shutter release unit. The only modification was to attach a small button (or cardboard disc) approximately 10 mm (1/2 in) in diameter to the end of the narrow rod which triggers the camera shutter when the rubber ball is squeezed. The disc was fixed to the rod using silicone sealer which is both flexible and adhesive.

On squeezing the rubber ball, the disc taps the puff-ball causing it to release a cloud of spores. Almost simultaneously the cable release was pressed, tripping the shutter and firing the flash units. The main difficulties were squeezing the rubber ball just sufficiently to produce a well-formed cloud of spores and triggering the camera shutter and flash units at exactly the right moment to capture the spore cloud.

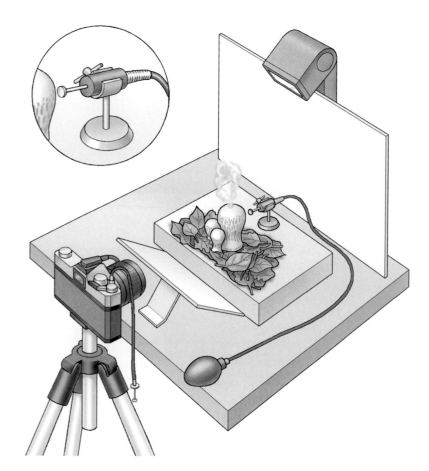

The 90mm macro lens was set at f 22 for maximum depth of field and on aperture priority with the exposure reduced by −1 stop in 1/3 stop increments to ensure a well exposed transparency. The Kodak Ektachrome 64 film was set at ISO 80.

This is a fascinating but quite tricky exercise calling for great care in setting up the puff-balls and the mechanical 'tapper'. But with a little patience it can be done and one good result showing a sharply defined, well-composed cloud of spores will be ample reward for all your efforts.

EQUIPMENT

OLYMPUS OM2n

90MM MACRO LENS

T32 AND T20 FLASH UNITS

WHITE CARD REFLECTOR

BACKGROUND BOARD

TRIPOD AND CABLE RELEASE

KODAK EKTACHROME 64 FILM

This was one of the later shots taken with more side/backlighting and a white reflector in front, approximately 15cm (6in) from the puff-balls.

The photograph has immediate impact with the cloud of spores highlighted against the dark background. The composition is satisfactory with the eye following the dead leaves and twigs up the gradient past the two smaller puff-balls to the 'blow-hole' on the top of the main specimen. The exposure was made at just about the right moment (or possibly a few milliseconds too early), capturing a well-defined cloud of spores. The strong backlighting has paid off handsomely allowing the spore cloud to stand out really well against the dark background. (Under daylight or frontal flash lighting the spore cloud is barely visible.)

The dark, predominantly brown background suits the mood, adding a solid frame to the picture. Exposure: flash, f 22, aperture priority with –2/3 stop underexposure.
90mm macro lens. Kodak Ektachrome 64.

TIPS

❖ Patience is more important than equipment in this assignment.

❖ Collect ripe puff-balls already packed with spores – a gentle tap will verify this.

❖ Keep repeating the shots – be prepared to use at least half a roll of film in an attempt to capture the perfect spore cloud.

SYCAMORE FRUIT DISPERSAL

The aim of this indoor workshop is to try to illustrate the rotating movement of the sycamore fruit as it spins down to the ground – simple in theory but more difficult in practice.

This assignment was carried out indoors in an area with a reasonable level of daylight. Sycamore fruits are available from June until October but in the earlier ones the pericarp wings tend to be greenish and rather opaque while the later ones, having dried out, have large, translucent, membranous wings. The material was collected and the photographs taken in late September.

The camera was focused on the sycamore fruit suspended on a length of black cotton thread and located in the upper quarter of the frame. The sycamore, previously wound up like a propeller, was released and as it rotated and came face on to the camera the shutter was tripped. First the flash was fired and then during a one-second exposure the camera was slowly and smoothly tilted upwards to a pre-set stopping point with the sycamore just out of frame. The flash produced a nice sharp, well-lit image of the sycamore fruit while the slow tilt put a vortex-like swirl on the transparency. After processing, the transparency was turned upside down, showing the sycamore heavy-end down, slowly spinning to the ground.

There were three problems – finding the right balance between the continuous lighting producing the swirl effect and the flash illuminating the sycamore fruit; firing the flash at the best moment and panning very smoothly and at the right speed during the one second exposure.

The fruit and the background were lit using a 60 watt domestic bulb in an angle-poise reading lamp but to get rid of some of the yellow cast from the bulb (too low a colour temperature) I held a piece of pale blue celluloid over the lamp during the exposure.

With the camera set on manual and the shutter speed at one second, the suggested aperture was f 8 which I set at f 11 (with 2/3 stop bracketing either side) to obtain a darker background. I rolled up a piece of black cartridge paper to produce a 25 cm (10 in) long snook and attached it to the T32 flash unit. This would prevent any spillage of light onto the background. The flash unit was set at quarter strength on 'manual' and used at distances varying from 45 to 65 cm. The one second exposure was used as it was the longest available on the Olympus OM2n camera in the 'manual' mode and it gave me just sufficient time for the smooth tilting upswing of the camera.

This is one of the trickiest assignments in the book, with difficult to control variables, such as the speed of rotation of the wings, the smoothness of the vertical panning and picking the right moment to fire the flash, all producing their own problems. But at least the set-up is quite simple and if you are prepared to experiment, you should be able to produce some acceptable images.

EQUIPMENT

OLYMPUS OM2n

50MM MACRO LENS

T32 FLASH UNIT

60 WATT HOUSEHOLD BULB
IN ANGLE-POISE LAMP

TRIPOD WITH A PAN AND TILT HEAD,

PAINTED BACKGROUND CARD

SMALL LABORATORY STAND

BLACK COTTON

SHEET OF BLACK CARTRIDGE PAPER

TIPS

❖ Lots of patience needed for this assignment.

❖ Use the last few exposures on a previous film to test the set-up, varying the aperture and flash distance.

❖ Be prepared to use plenty of film – success rate is low.

❖ Good luck!

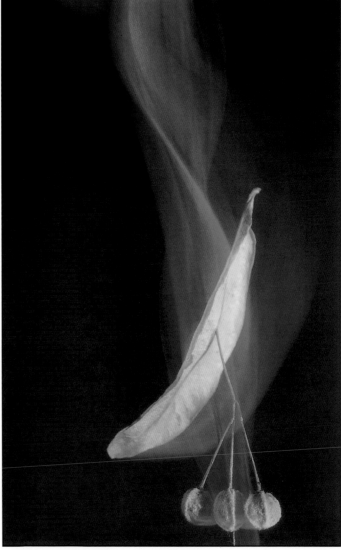

The composition although simple is satisfactory with the vortex swirling slightly to the right suggesting motion. It stands out quite well against the dark olive green background with an interesting cross-over point near to the centre of the picture. The sycamore fruit, positioned slightly off centre and with a small amount of tilt on it, lies parallel to the film plane resulting in tip to tip sharpness across the wings. The shot would have been improved slightly if the swirl had been visible at the tip of the left wing.

Exposure: 1 sec, f 11, flash, −2/3 stop underexposure. 50mm macro lens. Kodak Elite 100.

After having had some success with the sycamore fruit I repeated it using lime, which consists of two or three hard yellowy fruits attached via a long stalk to a leaf-like bract. The selected image shows a double spiral; the wider one produced by the rotating bract with the narrow spiral marking the descent of the fruit. Compositionally it would have looked more attractive if the descent had been diagonal although in nature this only happens when a strong wind is blowing; normally the descent is vertical as illustrated. The set-up, camera, light position and exposure were the same as in the sycamore photograph.

SWEET CHESTNUTS

The aim of this assignment is to produce a sharply defined, well-composed image of a carpet of sweet chestnuts when viewed from above.

The male catkins hang from the bases of leaf stalks on the younger shoots while the inconspicuous greenish female flowers develop at the base of the catkin and are usually in groups of three set in a small prickly collar (cupule). Pollination is by wind or insects and after fertilisation the cupule grows around the developing nuts to form the familiar spiny 'hedgehog' outer coat. Some of the spiny fruit remain on the tree and the coat splits open with the four lobes peeling back to expose up to three glossy brown nuts packed snugly together. Other fruits fall to the ground and split open on the carpet of fallen leaves.

The British sweet chestnuts are small compared to those imported from Spain, nevertheless they are still very tasty when roasted.

I visit this area of woodland almost daily when walking our dog, keeping a close eye on the seasonal changes in the tree and shrub population. It was early October.

The ground was well covered with chestnuts in their spiny coats, but the viewfinder image indicated that one or two nuts needed repositioning slightly as they were being cut in half by the edges of the frame. As the light was quite bright but slightly diffused, no additional lighting was employed. Several exposures were made using aperture priority, bracketing the exposures 1/3 stop either side.

To obtain a different angle on the chestnuts, several with the leaves on which they were lying were collected and arranged on a tray in the conservatory at home. The tray was tilted to around 20°, with the camera kept horizontal to photograph the chestnuts in side-view rather than from above. Realising there might be a depth-of-field problem, I limited the depth of the set to around 20 cm (8 in) and stopped down the lens to f 22. A photograph taken in the woods some weeks earlier was enlarged and used as a background. Because the lighting in the conservatory was rather flat and diffused, a hand-held, pale blue filtered video light provided a little contrast and modelling.

This is a straightforward piece of work, well within the competence of any nature photographer, but there might be a problem finding a sweet chestnut tree. It is worth checking local parks and estates; fortunately the tree is easily identified by its, often, twisted trunk, highly fissured bark and the large-toothed margins of the spearhead-shaped leaves.

EQUIPMENT

BRONICA ETRSi

100MM MACRO LENS

E-28 EXTENSION TUBE

TRIPOD AND CABLE RELEASE

KODAK ELITE ISO 100 FILM.

Sweet chestnuts in side view with the depth of field just about adequate. The overall lighting is satisfactory while the background looks quite natural, but somehow the picture doesn't quite gel. Is the arrangement a little too haphazard for a well-composed photograph and are the leaves at the top right too dominant? However the photograph looks natural and does not betray the fact that it was set up and photographed indoors. Exposure: 1/2 sec, f 22. 100mm macro lens. Extension tube. Kodak Elite 100.

This arrangement was housed in the conservatory and was an attempt to photograph the chestnuts in side view. Daylight was the main source of the lighting with a hand-held video light providing a little contrast.

This photograph seems to have worked quite well with a good display of shiny brown chestnuts well spread across the frame. There are several snugly packed groups of three interspersed among pairs and singles, with a variety of interesting shapes formed by the curled-back spiny coats. I had to move slightly one or two chestnuts which were being eye-catchingly cropped by the edges of the frame but I hope the arrangement still looks quite natural. The harmonising creams, browns and greens of the chestnuts and their spiny cases fit in well with the rich dark brown of the sweet chestnut leaves forming the background. Exposure: 1/8 sec, f 22. 100mm macro lens. Extension tube. Kodak Elite 100.

TIPS

❖ Select undamaged examples and include some three-nut arrangements.

❖ Ideal lighting – bright sky with thin cloud – not too contrasty.

❖ Set the camera film plane parallel to the spread of chestnuts. Use a small aperture to produce good depth of field – inherently shallow in close-up work.

AUTUMN LEAVES

The purpose of this mainly indoor workshop is to evoke the feelings of a balmy autumn morning after overnight rain, through the medium of fallen autumn leaves.

In autumn the leaves of deciduous trees change from a tired-looking dark green to a whole range of wonderful golds, oranges and reds, completely transforming the countryside. As the ground becomes cold and water freezes, the roots have difficulty obtaining sufficient water and if the leaves continued to lose water, the tree or shrub would wilt and eventually die. The leaves are shed and the tree allowed to go dormant over the winter.

The green chlorophylls are broken down, and the useful products (carotenoids) are transported out of the leaf. The remaining materials and the yellow pigments previously masked by the chlorophyll, plus the red colours produced by the breakdown of leaf starches, form the familiar autumn tints.

Several attempts were made to photograph autumn leaves on the ground in situ but the results were disappointing as the light was never as I wanted. I therefore decided to collect some leaves and set them up in the controlled environment of our kitchen. The leaves were scattered haphazardly on the table as they might have fallen from the tree but the viewfinder only revealed an unattractive haphazard scattering of leaves!

After much searching, I found an attractive, undamaged leaf which would form the centrepiece of the picture. Arranging the set proved quite difficult as I tried to achieve good composition which still looked natural.

The lighting in the kitchen consisted of low level cloudy daylight combined with overhead fluorescent lighting. As it was obviously too flat, I set up a slide projector approximately 90 cm (36 in) away, pointing down at an angle of 35°, to produce strong side lighting. Several exposures were made by first using the projector light unfiltered (colour temperature around 3500 Kelvin and therefore towards the warm end of the colour temperature scale), followed by a single, then a double thickness of pale blue acetate sheet. Finally I tried a blue 80A colour conversion filter.

The processed film showed a gradation from the rather yellow 'autumn light' of the unfiltered projector lamp through the slightly cooler colours to the over compensated effect of the 80A blue filter. But the images still lacked that sparkle needed to lift them above the 'average', so using a syringe I carefully applied drops of water to several leaves and rephotographed them.

This is an absorbing indoor workshop assignment, particularly if you like to experiment. If a slide projector is unavailable, any strong directional lighting from, for example, a spotlight (photographic or motor car) will suffice. Spend time on the composition as it is basically a flat two-dimensional image relying mainly on graphic design.

EQUIPMENT

BRONICA ETRSI

100MM MACRO LENS

TRIPOD

SLIDE PROJECTOR

SELECTION OF BLUE FILTERS.

This shot of ornamental maple leaves was taken outdoors under the tree after a wet night. The leaves were rearranged a little to achieve a more attractive composition but the final image is still lacking that special quality we are always striving to achieve. Exposure: 1/30 sec, f 16. 90mm macro lens. Fuji Sensia 100.

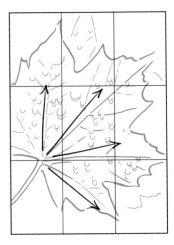

The eye is attracted to the junction of the leaf stalk and the leaf blade of the Norway maple which is located at the strong point of the 'rule of thirds'. The eye then follows the leaf veins as they fan out across the frame from left to right, with the left vein almost parallel to the side of the picture. I used the underside of the leaf because the veins are more prominent, accentuated by the grazed lighting. The leaves around and under the central leaf are a darker brown forming a natural frame to the picture and allowing the eye to concentrate on the central leaf. Finally the jewel-like droplets of water with their well-defined shadows add the finishing touch to this pleasing picture. Exposure: 4 sec, f 22. 100mm macro lens. Fuji Provia 100.

TIPS

❖ Collect undamaged leaves with well-defined veins.

❖ Choose the best leaf and sponge off the 'dirt'.

❖ Water droplets can be applied with a fine medicine dropper or a syringe but the leaf surface must be dry and glossy otherwise droplets will spread.

❖ A slide projector produces a high contrast beam, but some blue filtration must be added to raise the colour temperature.

CHAPTER SEVEN

Mammals

Hedgehogs, field mice, squirrels, foxes, deer, badgers and many other creatures including all birds are warm-blooded (homeothermic) in contrast to fish, frogs and snakes which are cold-blooded (poikilothermic).

Warm-blooded animals have a high constant temperature of 37°C - 40°C (98°F - 104°F) which gives them two great advantages over their cold-blooded brethren. The body's chemical reactions can proceed at a brisk pace making them efficient, quick and alert; it also enables them to successfully colonise areas of temperature extremes such as polar regions and tropical plains and forests. The disadvantages are that in cold weather warm-blooded animals have to generate large quantities of heat energy, requiring regular feeding, to maintain their high body temperature, while in very hot regions they must get rid of excess heat, mainly through sweating, to prevent overheating.

Most warm-blooded animals are active all the year round, but grey squirrels are less active in the winter, badgers spend more time in their underground setts (yet both must come out to feed), while hedgehogs lay up lots of body fat in the autumn to carry them through their winter hibernation. Resident birds must feed very regularly and frequently during the cold winter weather to provide sufficient energy to maintain their high body temperature, whereas migratory birds move to warmer climates, with a more plentiful food supply, as winter approaches.

Badgers are warm-blooded but being larger and bulkier than say a vole or field mouse, they have a smaller surface area to volume ratio, losing less heat through the body surface. However badgers still have to spend many hours during the late evening and night foraging for food which includes a large variety of animals and plants, particularly earth worms, consuming up to 200 each night. They also spend more time during the winter in the warmth and protection of their underground setts. Exposure: flash, f8. 75-300mm lens. Fuji Sensia 100.

The hedgehog is in the early stages of uncurling. The composition rather breaks the rules in that the subject displays perfect bilateral symmetry with the main areas of interest right in the lower centre of the frame. A good camera angle (plus a little luck) resulted in the nose, both sets of claws, most of the spines and even the black whiskers all being in sharp focus. But because the hedgehog is just beginning to uncurl, the eyes are still in deep shadow, protected by the spines and coarse hair – a natural position but not ideal from a photographic viewpoint. Exposure: flash, f22. 100mm macro lens. Extension tube. Close-up lens. Fuji Velvia.

THE RED SQUIRREL

Location Workshop

What we are trying to produce in this assignment are some appealing images of red squirrels going about their normal daily activities.

I had been watching the evening weather forecast for the Lancashire coast for several days and when 'dry and sunny' flashed up on the TV screen I packed my equipment and set off for Formby Point early the following morning. Six hours were spent there but the sun never made an appearance; just overcast conditions, but thankfully no rain. The exercise was repeated some three weeks later and exactly the same thing happened – overcast and no sun. Weather forecasting is obviously not a very exact science!

I mention this because trying to photograph very active squirrels requires a shutter speed of at least 1/125 sec but I had to be content with 1/8–1/30 sec at f 5.6 on ISO 100 film and 1/30–1/60 on the faster film in the Minolta camera.

Wanting to shoot at ground level rather than looking down at the squirrels, I found a banked area with an almost flat top on the edge of the pine wood where there was also maximum light. The Olympus camera was set up on the tripod with the ball and socket half-tightened to give support but sufficiently slack to allow camera movement when necessary. The Minolta autofocus camera with its 400mm f 5.6 lens was attached to the monopod to allow easy movement but mainly to give support as I had to use too slow shutter speeds for a 400mm lens.

Settling down at the bottom of the low bank, I rattled the food bag and threw nuts up into the air trying to bounce them off the trunks of the nearby pines (noise will attract the squirrels). After about 20 minutes a squirrel arrived, looked cautiously around, picked up a nut, moved about 20 feet away and quickly buried it. This was repeated several times before the squirrel started to nibble one of the nuts; by which time one or two other squirrels had joined the party. I was in business at last!

This is not an easy project because the red squirrel is a very active animal, only coming near you to feed. This involves vigorous head and claw movements as the food is hungrily consumed. You have to balance shutter speed and lens aperture, with the added problem of camera shake when using a 400mm lens.

The image is sharp with the squirrel well positioned in the frame and looking slightly to the left into the space available. The eye is bright and sharp with a catchlight which gives it added life. The paws and claws are clearly defined and although the hazelnut is not visible its presence is implied.

On the negative side, the squirrel looks slightly hunched up, his ear tufts could be longer and his tail is not in the classic 'up' position. Exposure: 1/15 sec, f 5.6. 75–300 lens. Kodak Elite 100.

EQUIPMENT

OLYMPUS OM2n

75–300 TELEPHOTO LENS

MINOLTA 7000i

400MM LENS

TRIPOD AND MONOPOD

KODAK ELITE 100

KODAK ELITE 200

HAZELNUTS AND PEANUTS.

A squirrel snuggled into the side of a pine trunk quietly enjoying a nut. Again it remained there for only a few seconds but long enough to capture this attractive image. I particularly like the long, well developed brush-like tail. Exposure: 1/30 sec, f 5.6. 400mm lens. Kodak Elite 200

A 'snatched' shot taken as the young squirrel paused momentarily on its way up a tree chased by another squirrel. The position of the squirrel is good with space above it to move into but as a consequence the end of the tail has been lost, which is a pity. Backlighting has put an attractive rim of light around the squirrel but there is still some detail in its coat and a catchlight in the eye. The streak down the right side of the picture is a little distracting but at least it is fairly dark and overall I'm pleased with the result. Exposure: 1/30 sec, f 5.6. 400mm autofocus lens. Kodak Elite 200.

TIPS

❖ Select terrain which allows you to shoot at ground level – image is more attractive and intimate.

❖ Use a tripod for static shots and a monopod for moving shots, both with half-tightened ball-and-socket heads – gives some freedom and support.

❖ Don't forget the food supply – hazelnuts or peanuts – otherwise squirrels won't come near you. They're not stupid!

DEER

A large deer park will, hopefully, prove a happy hunting ground for the production of some fairly close-up images of various species of deer.

Most deer are forest dwellers and are widely distributed throughout Europe, Asia, North America and the Far East. The deer family also includes reindeer and elks, known as caribou and moose in North America.

To photograph wild deer in, for example, the Scottish Highlands requires lots of time, patience and local knowledge, and even then success can never be guaranteed. A more reliable alternative is to visit a large deer park such as the huge 600 acre park at Studley Royal in North Yorkshire. It was early September just before the rutting season got under way, but during my first two visits the deer were nowhere to be seen. However my third attempt looked promising as a large herd was grazing some quarter of a mile (400 m) away.

They were feeding and moving very slowly as a group, but occasionally, for no obvious reason (to me at least), they would break into a trot and then settle down to graze again. Apparently they are unable to identify distant stationary objects but the slightest movement is detected instantly, while their constantly twitching ears and well-developed sense of smell immediately warn them of potential danger.

Electing to travel as light as possible, I selected a couple of lenses (500mm APO and 75–300mm zoom) plus the camera body and a large Benbo tripod. The weather was dry and sunny with no wind to carry the 'scent' as I started to close in on the herd, using the cover provided by bushes and dips in the terrain but each time I stood upright to check on their whereabouts the herd had quietly moved on, always keeping a safe 100 metres or so from me. I did not take any photographs!

Spotting another group, I managed to work my way around and towards them using some woodland as cover. The deer had crossed a stream and were high up on the opposite hillside.

EQUIPMENT

OLYMPUS OM2n

500 MM APO LENS

TRIPOD AND BEANBAG

A male sika deer sporting an impressive pair of antlers and fine mane as the rutting season approaches. Well placed in the frame with an out of focus background, this almost rear view shot is only acceptable because the deer's head is turned a little towards the camera. There is a small catchlight just visible in the eye. Exposure: 1/60 sec, f 11. 500mm APO lens. Kodak Ektachrome 200.

Crouching behind a dense bush, I set up the camera, lens and tripod and cautiously observed the deer opposite. Some looked up but not sensing any danger continued feeding. Several shots were taken, trying in particular to capture a red deer as it lifted its head and looked directly towards me. On my way back to the car I spotted a solitary sika deer sporting a fine pair of antlers, and he very obligingly stood still long enough for me to make several exposures.

Driving through the deer park towards the exit, I noticed a small fallow deer chewing the cud in the late afternoon sunshine. I switched off the engine and coasted along until the car was adjacent to the deer some 50 metres away. Sliding across the passenger seat, out of the door and onto the road, I quickly retrieved my camera from the back seat and not having time (so I thought) to set up the tripod, slowly slid a large beanbag onto the car roof and snuggled the camera and lens down onto it. Using the car as a hide, three shots were fired off before the deer got to its feet and trotted away to a safer, more distant feeding ground.

This is a good exercise in stalking 'wild' animals and if the necessary precautions, mentioned above, are taken, it should be possible for any competent nature photographer to get sufficiently close to obtain some attractive frame-filling images of individual deer. Lots of time and patience are the fundamental requirements for this type of work.

TIPS

❖ Take the minimum of equipment as you may have to do a lot of rough walking.

❖ Despite the suggestion above, a substantial tripod will help prevent camera shake when using a long lens (500 mm).

❖ Wear subdued, non-'rustly' clothing and keep downwind of the deer – they have a well developed sense of smell.

❖ If a deer looks up at you – freeze. They can't easily identify stationary objects.

A classic shot of a large red deer stag looking straight at the camera. The stag is well positioned in the frame with the dark grass forming a solid base to the picture. The afternoon sunlight is grazing the side of the stag, highlighting the texture of its coat while the almost perfectly symmetrical antlers are nicely lit against a plain light sky.

On the negative side, the sky is rather uninspiring but at least it allows the stag to stand out in an impressive way. Exposure: 1/30 sec, f 11. 500mm APO lens. Ektachrome 200.

THE BADGER

What we are hoping to do in this assignment is to produce interesting images of the badger in its natural environment, playing with its cubs, and finally in close-up if possible.

The obvious identifying feature is the triangular, black and white striped head and the white-edged ears. But whether the stripes help them to see each other in the sett or when out feeding we really don't know. Their sense of smell is extremely well developed; hearing is good but eyesight tends to be rather poor and, being very shy nocturnal animals, they leave the sett at sunset and return before dawn.

The sett is in a bank some 4 metres high and 200 metres long, being part of a drainage system in flat fen-like farmland.

Each visit followed the same pattern. We would choose a night when the breeze was blowing towards us from the sett and arrive at the small open-fronted shelter around 6.45 p.m. By 7.15 p.m. the tripod-mounted cameras and flash units were in position, after which we sat in complete silence until around 8.15 p.m. when the first badger would emerge from the sett. It moved its head from side to side sniffing the air and listening for signs of danger and, when satisfied that it was safe, would leave the sett followed a few seconds later by the cubs. This was all happening about 50 metres away.

On several occasions a badger came within 3 metres, raised his head and looked directly at me. I 'froze' and after a few seconds he got his head down again and resumed feeding. The flash units were set up in various positions, initially using just two units attached to the camera bracket, but later two were positioned to the left about 2 metres from the camera (and nearer to the badgers), using the third unit as a backlight some 6 metres away and slightly to the right. The badgers' response to the flash varied; one badger ignored it completely, while others bolted away and hid behind the pea crop, only to emerge a couple of minutes later and start feeding again.

The 75–300mm zoom lens was used at settings between 150 and 300mm with apertures from f 5.6 to f 11 depending on the distances between the badgers and the main flash units. The sessions usually ended around 9.15 p.m. when it became too dark to focus the camera. Any competent photographer should be able to produce images like this if he has a reasonable range of telephoto lenses, several powerful flash units and the ability to capture a good facial expression the split second it occurs.

EQUIPMENT

OLYMPUS OM2n

75–300MM ZOOM LENS

THREE METZ 45 FLASH UNITS

BENBO TRIPOD.

Two badgers in their natural environment, just below one of the sett entrances. I had to take this photograph quickly as the setting sun had already put some of the soft earth and much of the grass in shadow. There is a slight 'softness' on the head and ears of the nearest badger due to subject movement. This is the price you pay when using a longish exposure in low level sunlight. Exposure: 1/30 sec, f 5.6. 300 mm lens. Fuji Sensia 100.

❖ It is best to work with someone who has been visiting a sett regularly.

❖ Badgers have a very keen sense of smell – keep downwind of them.

❖ Their eyesight is poor – if one stops feeding and looks up at you, simply freeze, and it will soon start feeding again.

❖ Don't forget the food – they love peanuts. It's not their natural food so keep it out of sight of the camera.

The three badgers at the front are all in sharp focus with eye catchlights visible in two of them, with their coats backlit by a flash unit positioned approximately 3 metres behind them to the right. On the negative side, the third badger's head is partially masked by the pea crop and the rather puzzled-looking badger is not quite sharp, being just beyond the depth of field of the lens. Exposure: flash, f 8. 200mm lens setting. Fuji Sensia 100.

This is the close-up I had been hoping for all week. The badger was quite close (approx. two metres) to the main flash units on the left and about two metres from the camera. I quickly stopped down to f 11 to increase the depth of field, waiting until the badger looked up to check for incipient danger, before making the exposure. Fortunately its head and shoulders are almost parallel to the film plane resulting in excellent definition from the tip of the nose to the middle of the back. Again the backlight flash helped to highlight the texture of the fur while the small eye catchlight was an added bonus as the main flash units were to the left of the badger rather than directly in front of it. Exposure: flash, f 11. 135mm setting. Fuji Sensia 100. All the badger shots were taken in July and August on the Isle of Axholme, Humberside, England.

CHAPTER EIGHT

Rivers, Streams and Ponds

Most rivers begin life quite unobtrusively in, for example, a wet meadow, a bog or perhaps as a trickle of water emerging from clefts in a rock. The source of the mighty Thames is a damp patch in a field near Cirencester in the Cotswolds while the Severn and Wye rise close together in a bog on the north-eastern slopes of the Plynlimon mountain in North Wales. Tributaries of the Humber – the Swale, Ure, Nidd, Wharfe, Aire, Calder, Derwent and Don – rise on the eastern slopes of the Pennines, carrying most of their water across the Vale of York into the Ouse and finally to the Humber estuary and the North Sea.

Near its origins a river is little more than a shallow stream but as more streams combine, the river becomes wider, deeper and faster flowing, making it difficult for water plants to gain a hold (except around the quieter edges). The animal population consists of active swimmers such as freshwater shrimps and the nymphs of mayflies, stoneflies and caddis flies, which often live under stones for protection, and to prevent being carried downstream.

As the river loses height, waterfalls become a common feature. These can be identified on an Ordnance Survey map (2.5 in to 1 mile, 1:25000) where the contour lines, instead of running parallel to the river, suddenly join together and cross it. The height of the waterfall is indicated by the number of contour lines involved. In this part of the river water temperatures tend to be low but stable and, due to turbulence in the water, oxygen levels are high to the benefit of aquatic animal life.

Further downstream the river normally widens, becoming smoother and quieter as it reaches the flatter plains, while towards its mouth, brackish water produces its own special animal and plant populations. In the lower reaches there may be sheltered, or even cut off, areas of water where conditions are more akin to a pond. This is discussed later in the chapter.

Iceland is well known for its crystal clear atmosphere, its hot water springs, its grey/black volcanic rock and of course its numerous spectacular waterfalls. Exposure: 1/60 sec, f 11. 50mm lens. Kodak Gold.

Wooded river scene photographed at 7 a.m. in early June, with various shades of green reflected in the water producing a calm and tranquil atmosphere. There was some slight disturbance on the surface of the water, smoothed out by using a longish exposure. Exposure: 1/2 sec, f 22. 50mm lens. Kodak Ektachrome 100.

WATER OVER WEIR

The aim of this exercise is to photograph water rushing over a weir using a range of shutter speeds to produce different effects on the water.

Since 1880 the River Washburn, which rises on Pockstones Moor on the eastern slopes of the Pennines in North Yorkshire, has had no less than four reservoirs built into its valley to satisfy the ever increasing demand for water in the Leeds area.

From Thruscross, the highest reservoir, the Washburn runs south under the A59 Harrogate to Skipton road, into the Fewston reservoir. This short stretch of river, rough and fast moving in parts, but quiet and peaceful in other sections, supports an interesting bird population including grey wagtails, sand martins, dippers and the occasional brilliant kingfisher.

Midway along this part of the river is an old stone weir, which provided the location for this assignment. After arriving at the weir on an early November morning, I spent some time exploring the immediate area looking for a viewpoint which would produce a

well composed picture. As the sky was rather dull and overcast, a warming-up filter (85C) was used to brighten up the scene. With the lens fully open (f 2.8), the low light level indicated an exposure of 1/30 sec, which was not sufficiently short to completely 'freeze' the surging water. However there was no difficulty in smoothing out the surface of the water, as at f 22 the exposure was a lengthy 3 seconds. Both vertical and horizontal formats were used with the Bronica firmly mounted on a Benbo tripod and the shutter tripped using a cable release.

Any competent nature photographer can easily master this assignment but you will have to spend most of the time searching for a well-composed image. Choose bright weather if possible; this will allow you to use a short (1/60 sec or less) exposure to 'freeze' the water and a long exposure of several seconds (by stopping down the lens and if necessary adding a neutral density filter) to produce a smooth ethereal effect.

EQUIPMENT

BRONICA ETRSi

STANDARD 75MM LENS

BENBO TRIPOD

WARMING-UP FILTERS

FUJI PROVIA 100 FILM.

The water above the weir is quiet and tranquil, making it an ideal location for a family of mute swans. Exposure: 1/125 sec, f8. 75-300mm lens. Fuji Sensia 100.

Using a shortish exposure, the water is reasonably well 'frozen' but, due to the dull weather, the wide lens aperture resulted in a rather shallower-than-ideal depth of field, witness the out of focus foreground. The composition is satisfactory with the water flowing diagonally across the frame meeting the eye when the picture is viewed from the left (as when reading the printed word). Acceptable framing has been achieved with rock and grass at the bottom of the picture and middle and distance trees framing the two sides. I chose the vertical format as it gives the picture a more dynamic quality. Exposure: 1/30 sec, f 2.8. Bronica 75mm lens. 82C filter. Fuji Provia 100.

TIPS

❖ If possible have the water flowing diagonally through the frame – much more dynamic than 'horizontal' water.

❖ Experiment using a wide range of shutter speeds – each produces its own special effect which is unpredictable, in any detail, beforehand.

This shot was taken immediately after the one on the left, using a small lens aperture coupled to a long exposure. The most striking effect is the rendering of the water as a swirling mist, creating an ethereal effect, not normally seen by the human eye. In contrast to the soft misty water, the surrounding rocks and trees are pin-sharp, with the exception of a few green leaves and dead bracken at the bottom right which show signs of movement due to a slight breeze. The composition is the same as in the previous picture. Exposure: 3 sec, f 22. Bronica 75mm lens. 82C filter. Fuji Provia 100.

Aysgarth Falls

In this assignment we will be trying to capture the sheer beauty and power of the Aysgarth Falls, paying particular attention to composition and lighting.

My first visit to the falls in early May was little more than a reconnaissance to explore the lie of the land, but principally to decide the best time of day to take photographs, when the sun would light up not just the falls but the woodland on both sides of the fairly steep gorge.

Arriving at the lower falls, compass in hand, I soon realised that the trees on the south side of the waterfalls would be in deep shade by 10 a.m. The upper falls face south-east in a much more open setting, suggesting late morning as a good time to photograph them. (The middle falls were omitted, as they are not so spectacular and access is more difficult.)

The following week I made my second visit, leaving home at 5.30 a.m., arriving at Aysgarth at exactly 8 o'clock to discover the normally full car park completely empty. As there had been a lot of heavy rain during the previous few days, the river was in full spate with foaming water pouring over the limestone outcrops in a frenzied rush dragging tree branches and plant debris in its wake.

Moving downstream to the lower falls, I strolled around looking for suitable vantage points which would include not only the falls but also the 'boiling' water racing along within a few inches of my feet. The camera was tripod-mounted with exposures ranging from 1/8 sec to 1/125 sec to capture both 'smoothed-out' and 'angry' water. The sun shone brightly from a cloudless sky.

Packing up the equipment, I walked back upriver, past the middle falls to the bridge and main road near to the upper falls. With the sun almost on my back the more open landscape was well lit, as I looked round for suitable shooting points. After trying one or two, it soon became clear that the best shots could only be taken by standing on a pointed-topped stone wall with the road on one side and a sheer drop down to the river on the other. Very gingerly I climbed the wall and made two exposures, hand-holding the camera, before my nerve failed and I dropped down onto the road again. By midday it was all over.

This shot captures the essence of a multiple waterfall in full spate, but had there been much more water coming over, the individual falls would have merged into one and the rocks I was standing on would be totally submerged. The composition is good, with the falls located at a strong point in the frame (intersection of thirds) and the water flowing diagonally to the left. I chose the 1/60 sec shot because the swirling water in the foreground looks more powerful than completely 'frozen' water. The sun is just grazing some of the trees on the far bank which a few minutes later were in deep shade. Exposure: 1/60 sec, f 8. Mamiya 75mm lens. Fuji Provia 100.

EQUIPMENT

MAMIYA 6

STANDARD 75MM LENS

BENBO TRIPOD

FUJI PROVIA 100 FILM.

Hand-held shot taken from a precarious position on a pointed-topped stone wall with a huge drop immediately below. The falls are well positioned in the frame with the water flowing diagonally, suggesting dynamic action, and just sufficiently frozen to register its angry, turbulent surface. The trees in the foreground and to the left are attractively lit, standing out well against the dark water and balanced by those at the top right. These trees and leafy branches not only help to frame the waterfalls but also add depth to the picture. Exposure: 1/60 sec, f 11. Mamiya 75mm lens. Fuji Provia 100.

TIPS

❖ Reconnoitre beforehand if possible as the position of the sun is important particularly if the water drops into a steep-sided gorge, which might be lit for just an hour or two each day.

❖ As with any moving water, a wide range of shutter speeds will produce quite different effects.

❖ Time of the year might be important if the waterfall is in a wooded area, as the summer leaf canopy could block out much of the light.

❖ Concentrate on viewpoint, composition and lighting, choosing preferably spring or autumn when the wooded banks of the river are attractive but not oppressively dark with heavy green foliage.

THE GREY HERON

What we are hoping to do in this assignment is to approach a heron sufficiently close to produce a large frame-filling image of an alert bird.

Standing gaunt and motionless in the shallows of a marsh, the grey heron, Ardea cinerea, can easily be mistaken for a tree stump or a wooden post. It may look inert and almost comatose but it is an expert 'fisherman', standing stock still, often on one leg, with its head hunched down between its shoulders contemplating its next meal.On seeing suitable food, such as a fish, eel, frog or vole, its head shoots forwards and downwards on its long flexible neck piercing the prey with its sharp pickaxe bill. Small fish are swallowed headfirst; larger ones are stabbed repeatedly and taken to the bank where the flesh is picked from their bones. Occasionally a heron will grasp a large fish in its bill and fly off to a quiet spot to enjoy it.

I had been trying for some time to take a close-up photograph of a grey heron, but without success. During a recent holiday on the River Moselle in the west of Germany, I decided to make a concerted effort. After walking along the river bank, we caught sight of a heron some 200 metres away. As we approached the bird looked our way and flew another 100 metres or so along the river, but remained on our side.

Alone, I advanced very slowly and when within 30 metres spread the tripod legs and lined up the camera. I stopped down the lens from f 7.2 to f 11 and made the first exposure at 1/30 sec using a cable release to activate the shutter. Over the next 15 minutes I moved closer and closer, taking one or two shots until finally the image of the heron was suitably large and well framed in the camera viewfinder. Several exposures were made showing the heron in various positions ranging from being hunched up, through the classic pose with the head partially raised, to the fully extended head and neck as movement in the surrounding water caught the bird's attention. The weather was fine and bright but rather overcast, resulting in uniform if rather flat lighting.

The difficult part of this assignment is getting sufficiently close to the heron to obtain a reasonably large image. Herons have forward-located eyes providing excellent three-dimensional vision but the field of view is fairly narrow, suggesting an oblique rather than too frontal an approach.

EQUIPMENT

OLYMPUS OM2n

500MM TELEPHOTO LENS, TRIPOD

KODAK ELITE II

ISO 100 SET AT ISO 125.

The heron is just beginning to emerge from the tall grass. Taken some 30 metres away, the image is really too small – but it was a start. Exposure: 1/30 sec, f 11. 500mm lens. Kodak Elite 100.

TIPS

❖ Wear neutral-coloured clothing, move slowly and use the local vegetation as a hide.

❖ Using your longest lens take the first shots some distance away as this may be your only opportunity – a small image is better than no image!

❖ Move towards the bird with the camera already mounted on a tripod (legs extended) because, unless you are using very fast film, the camera should not be hand-held when working with a 500mm lens of modest aperture.

The heron, standing on one leg in the typical resting position with its head well down on the curved neck. As the bird is side on to the camera, the head, eyes and long bill are all in sharp focus. The grey and black body is well positioned in the lower section of the frame with space to the right for the bird to move into.
The green foliage background would have looked better further back and therefore out of focus; but it is sufficiently 'soft' to allow the bird to stand out. Exposure: 1/30 sec, f 11. 500mm lens. Kodak Elite 100.

The heron is in the 'alert' position with the head held high on the long stretched neck. The obvious difference between this and the previous shot is that the heron is looking to the left (I simply reversed the transparency). I think this has more impact because we tend to scan pages from the left with the eye following quite naturally along the heron's bill to the head and the all-important eye. The grass and foliage behind the heron's head and neck are further away and therefore slightly out of focus, allowing the bird to 'pop out'. Exposure: 1/30 sec, f 11. 500mm lens. Kodak Elite 100.

REFLECTIONS ON WATER

In this assignment we are concentrating on different types of reflected image on the surface of a large lake.

Water, whether it is the sea or freshwater rivers and lakes, has a unique visual and emotional quality which attracts people in general and photographers in particular.

On a perfectly still, windless day the surface of a lake will act like a mirror producing a perfect reflection, whereas the slightest wind will distort it. The position of the sun will determine how the shrubs and trees are lit which in turn dictates the contrast and detail in the reflection. Reflections are not only used as an element in a picture, but can on occasions become the dominant feature and the raison d'être for taking the photograph.

It was mid-January and I had to visit the selected lake three times in ten days before conditions were even approaching satisfactory. On my first visit, due I suspect to the altitude, the lake was frozen over (the water in the birdbath at home was not frozen), on the second visit it was snow covered, but my third attempt, a few days later, was more successful as the temperature had risen and the snow and ice had gone. The sun shone from a clear blue sky though there was just a hint of a light intermittent breeze.

As the previous visits had also been used for reconnaissance purposes, it soon became apparent that the best time of day for photography would be between 1.00 and 2.45 p.m. when the very low winter sun would be bathing the shrubs and trees on the opposite side of the lake in 'warm', almost horizontal sunlight.

Using several locations on the west side of the lake, a series of photographs were taken using exposures ranging from 1/125 to 4 seconds with apertures from f 2.8 to f 22. On a couple of occasions a neutral density filter was used to cut down the light level and allow an even longer exposure. In this assignment I was not interested in looking below the surface of the water and therefore a polarising filter was definitely not required.

This is a fairly straightforward exercise with sunny calm weather being the key requirement. Vary the shutter speed to produce different effects and experiment with the ratio of reflected water to land. As ever, take time to achieve good composition.

In this shot I was trying to capture a perfect mirror image, making the exposure when the surface of the water was at its calmest. The water on the nearside of the lake is undisturbed providing an excellent mirror for the blue sky, clouds and tops of the trees, but further away it is disturbed slightly although the reflections are still reasonably good. From a compositional viewpoint the lake edge ('horizon') is at the 'intersection of thirds', with the area of tree-lined reflection increasing to the left, balanced by the grass and twigs at the bottom right. Useful framing is produced by the largely unlit twigs and branches near to the camera. A criticism could be that the vegetation at the bottom right is not sharply defined, but I had to strike a balance between the lens aperture (depth of field) and a reasonably short shutter speed. Exposure: 1/15 sec, f 9.5. 75mm lens. Fuji Velvia.

EQUIPMENT

PENTAX 645N

STANDARD 75MM LENS

X2 CONVERTER

TRIPOD

X2 NEUTRAL DENSITY FILTER

FUJI VELVIA ISO 50 FILM.

This photograph was taken to show that a smooth, but unsharp, reflection can be produced even when the surface of the water is disturbed, by giving a long exposure. A very small lens aperture was linked to a long exposure, extended by holding a neutral density filter in front of the lens. Exposure: 4 sec, f 22. 75mm lens. x2 converter, x2 neutral density filter. Fuji Velvia.

TIPS

❖ Best recipe for a good mirror-quality reflection is a completely windless day with plenty of bright sunlight and a clear blue sky.

❖ When photographing a reflection in a mirror or in water, always focus on the reflected image and not on the surface of the mirror or water – strange but true.

POND LIFE

Location Workshop

A pond is a bustling living community; a symbiotic association of plants and animals each dependent on the other, yet each striving to find a niche for itself where it can grow and reproduce successfully.

The type of pond which is likely to produce the best results for the nature photographer should be located in a quiet, secluded spot, free from the daily disturbance by children fishing for sticklebacks and newts. The pond should contain a rich variety of water plants including the less conspicuous but widespread filamentous green algae. This lies just below the surface resembling tufts of green cotton wool but when magnified reveals a beauty almost beyond words. Any pond with a healthy plant population is likely to support a rich variety of small creatures from minnow-sized fish right down to microscopic water fleas and rotifers.

That life evolved in water is no great surprise as it exhibits many characteristics which favour the growth of tiny organisms. An obvious, but often overlooked one, is that the very 'wetness' of water prevents animals and plants from drying out and dying from desiccation (unless the pond dries up completely).

The 'bulkiness' or density of water can support and buoy up small, fragile animals and plants which would collapse on dry land. The high thermal capacity of water results in a long cooling down and warming up period and while air temperatures can fluctuate wildly, water temperatures remain fairly constant, to the benefit of the organisms living there.

The surface of the water behaves like a delicate skin or elastic membrane supporting tiny, lightweight creatures such as pond skaters and whirligig beetles, which often have water repellent undersides or pads. Other insects make use of the underside of the surface film to hold them at the surface. Examples include the water boatman, water beetles and the larvae of mosquitoes and crane flies. All have one requirement in common: the necessity to come to the surface for air.

At some point in the food cycle, all animals are dependent on plants for food and therefore a pond devoid of plants will not support an animal population. Plants manufacture food by photosynthesis using carbon dioxide, water and sunlight trapped by green chlorophyll. A by-product of the process is oxygen, which animals and plants need to breathe, resulting in a long-term balance of the two gases.

Water also contains a mixture of nitrates, sulphates, chlorides, sodium, potassium and calcium, which are important to both plants and animals.

In this series of assignments on pond life, I have selected a few fairly representative animals and plants both large and small, including frogs and newts right down to microscopically small water fleas like Daphnia and Cyclops and the exquisitely sculptured diatoms and desmids. Most of these are indoor workshop projects and are covered in chapter ten (page 130).

A net can be used to catch fish and other free swimming creatures but here it is being used to concentrate all the tiny living organisms in many litres of water. By making several slow sweeps through the clearer water, tiny creatures collect in the glass tube as the water passes through the net.

A perfect pond consisting of a large area of sunlit water surrounded by a good range of trees and bushes plus an abundance of water plants. This is a perfect habitat for a very wide range of creatures including butterflies, damselflies, dragonflies, frogs, newts, various types of fish and a myriad of tiny pond creatures.

DAMSELFLY

Pin-sharp images of not one, but two, damselflies resting momentarily on grass stems around a large lake is the goal of this absorbing piece of outdoor photography.

In both the male and female the genital opening is located near the tip of the abdomen but before mating, the male transfers some sperm to a pouch on the underside of the abdomen just behind the thorax. On finding a female he arches his abdomen, grasping her in the 'neck' region using his anal claspers. When mating is about to take place, the female bends her body forwards under the male, picking up sperm from his sperm pouch. The pair can often be seen flying around hooked up in a heart-shaped formation.

I had to choose my day very carefully; ideally very bright sunshine softened slightly by a light haze or thin wispy cloud. Maximum light was essential because working at around half life size would require the smallest aperture commensurate with the shortest possible shutter speed, using a hand-held monopod-mounted camera.

It had to be a completely still, windless day, as I'd learnt from bitter experience that the slightest breath of wind could sway the grass stems and damselflies in and out of focus, making photography virtually impossible. On discovering a pair of damselflies in tandem resting on a stem or leaf, the monopod leg was adjusted to the appropriate length and the ball-and-socket head half-tightened to give adequate camera support but to allow some movement of the camera when grasped firmly in both hands.

I decided to use the 80mm Olympus Zuiko macro lens, which produces its best resolution around half- to twice-life size, mounted on a sliding automatic focusing tube.

As the damselfly has a very long, thin body and wings, getting the whole length and wings in sharp focus was not easy, requiring the film plane (i.e. camera back) to be absolutely parallel to the damselfly's body and wings. Hoping to photograph two damselflies more than doubled the problem. Holding the camera firmly with both hands, I moved in on the mating pair and, when everything looked satisfactory, squeezed the cable release. Exposures between 1/15 and 1/60 sec were used depending on the light level, realising, in theory at least, that the exposures were too long when using an 80mm lens at highish magnification.

EQUIPMENT

OLYMPUS OM2n

80MM ZUIKO MACRO LENS

OLYMPUS TELESCOPIC
AUTO TUBE 65–116

MONOPOD AND CABLE RELEASE

KODAK ELITE ISO 100 FILM

Left and above: Both insects are bitingly sharp with the female clasped firmly round the 'neck' by the male, leaving her suspended in mid-air. Mating is in progress with the tip of the female's abdomen in contact with the male's sperm sac.

The lighting is soft and pleasant with no hard shadows, and the fairly uniform background is sufficiently out of focus not to be a distraction. I think the colour contrast between the brown and blue insect bodies and the variegated green background works well. In both photographs the 80mm Zuiko macro lens had proved its worth. Exposure: 1/30 sec, f 16. 80mm macro lens. Kodak Elite 100.

TIPS

❖ Requires high light level without too much contrast – bright sun with thin, wispy clouds is ideal.

❖ Must be a still, wind-free day – even the slightest movement of the grass will throw the damselflies right out of focus.

❖ Angle the camera so that the film plane (camera back) is parallel to the main plane of the insects, ensuring that the bodies and wings are as sharp as possible.

❖ Check that there are no grass blades or stems immediately behind the damselflies – looks quite natural in the field but could spoil the background on an otherwise good photograph.

COMMON FROG

In this exercise we are hoping to photograph a pair of mating frogs plus a close-up portrait.

Widespread throughout Britain, Ireland and most of Northern Europe, the common frog, Rana temporaria, is too well known to warrant a description, but one or two interesting features are worth mentioning.

For example, a frog's hind legs, which include the greatly lengthened tarsals (ankle bones), are one and a half times longer than the body and can propel the frog some six to seven times its own body length, equivalent to a man leaping more than 30 ft from a standing start!

When feeding on small, moving creatures such as worms, flies, beetles, slugs and caterpillars, the frog flicks out its tongue, which, rather surprisingly, is hinged at the front of the mouth with the free end hanging down its throat. The tip of the flicked-out tongue curls around the prey and pulls it back into the mouth where it is held by small conical teeth on the upper jaw and palate. The prey is swallowed whole, aided by the large eyeballs which sink down into the head, giving the food an extra push!

It was early in April and the frogs were very active in a small pond in a friend's garden. I wanted to take some shots of frogs in amplexus (mating), starting with more distant images and then coming in much closer.

As I approached the edge of the pond with the tripod-mounted camera, the eight or so pairs of frogs immediately disappeared to the bottom, taking quarter of an hour or so before they slowly surfaced again. The main problem was matching the position of the frogs to the direction of the light, but all I could do was to remain quite still, slowly locating various pairs of frogs in the camera viewfinder. A series of shots were taken using the full range of the 75–300mm zoom lens. Being aware of the relatively shallow depth of field, particularly at the 300mm setting, as much of the frog as possible was kept parallel to the film plane, using the smallest aperture commensurate with a reasonably short exposure.

One or two shots were taken using a polarising filter to reduce surface reflections, but at the expense of losing up to two stops of light or lengthening the exposure by a factor of four.

EQUIPMENT

OLYMPUS OM2n

75–300 ZOOM LENS

AQUARIUM

TRIPOD

POLARISING FILTER

KODAK ELITE 50 FILM

In this shot a polarising filter was used to reduce the distracting reflections on the surfaces of the spawn. The penalty was a loss of 2 stops of light. Exposure: 1/4 sec, f 8. 75-300mm lens. Kodak Elite 50.

The two perfectly stacked frogs are tilted slightly
and placed off centre to make a more interesting
composition. As the upper frog was just behind the
lower one, I had to tilt the camera so that the film
plane was parallel to the two pairs of eyes,
ensuring all four were in sharp focus. The large
pupils surrounded by white-rimmed, gold-flecked
irises, command attention and although flash was
not used, catchlights are visible in two of the eyes.

A criticism might be that the tips of the digits of
the lower frog have been cropped slightly, while
the frog-spawn and water looks rather artificial.
Exposure: 1/8 sec, f 11. 75-300mm lens set at the
300mm end. Kodak Elite 50.

CHAPTER NINE

Gardens

The great advantage of taking photographs in the garden is its outstanding convenience. The camera, tripod and flash units need only be carried a few yards and can be assembled and left for several hours or even overnight in the knowledge that they will be safe and secure.

A mains power supply is readily available and, using extension leads, can reach the outer limits of even the largest garden, allowing lighting and mains-powered flash units, autowinders etc. to be used. Most equipment nowadays will run on batteries, but mains power (via mains adapters) can be a definite advantage when equipment has to be left switched on for several hours or right through the night. In cold weather you are always within easy reach of food, warmth and the bathroom, and if the weather deteriorates you can quickly retreat indoors. The final but most important benefit of using a well-stocked garden for photography is that plants, flowers and animals are on hand and don't have to be collected, carefully packed and transported back to base with the possibility of damage.

Plant and animal assignments covered in this section include hoar-frost on roses, tulips in the rain, garden birds in winter, grey squirrels, foxes at night, hedgehog uncurling and a spider in its web. The garden is also home to several plants and animals which I found more convenient to photograph indoors; these are discussed in the next chapter.

The sparrowhawk, Accipiter nisus, a regular visitor to our garden, seen here feeding on a recently caught pigeon. Using a 500mm lens I managed to get two shots before it saw me and flew away with the carcass. Exposure: 1/30sec, f7.2, Kodak Elite 100.

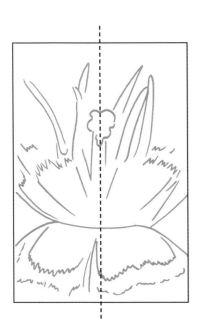

This is an example of bilateral symmetry in which an imaginary vertical line drawn down the centre of the frame produces a pair of almost identical images, with the three stamens and even the yellow and brown petal markings on the left mirrored by similar ones on the right. The long, pointed stamens are ripe, with tiny pollen grains visible on the top of the pistil; all kept in sharp focus using the lens well stopped down. The image is well balanced with the heavier tones in the lower part of the frame, while the red pigment towards the top is echoed by a similar hue running along the lower edge of the frame.
Exposure: 1 sec, f 32, –2/3 stop underexposure. 90 mm macro lens. Kodak Elite 50.

TULIPS

T he aims of this garden workshop are twofold: to produce well-lit images of tulips in the rain and to investigate the structure of a tulip flower in close-up.

Tulips probably originated as small wild species in the Middle East and by the sixteenth century had become popular European flowers. Holland soon became the centre for growing and hybridising a rich variety of form and colour with newly developed bulbs of rare-coloured flowers fetching high prices. Large-scale production of tulips for commercial purposes still continues in Holland today, with East Anglia being Britain's only significant tulip growing region.

The first part of the assignment was to photograph tulips in the rain but rather than wait for wet weather with its accompanying gloomy, overcast skies, I opted to make my own rain. Wanting all the flowers in sharp focus, my original idea of a naturally arranged bunch quickly gave way to a naturally arranged row, with the stems neatly taped to a length of wood.

Although the weather was quite bright (but not sunny), a 1000 watt mains voltage lamp (an old open-fronted model bought many years ago) was attached to a tall tripod to the right of the flowers, and tilted down to produce 45° side/back lighting. Water from a watering can was sprinkled down onto the flowers, and I triggered the camera shutter via a simple bell-push switch linked through household twin electrical flex to the 2.5mm jack-plug socket on the camera autowinder.

After making several exposures against the natural background of bushes and brick wall, a paint-sprayed background board was placed behind the flowers. Shutter speeds ranged from 1/8 to 1/60 sec to produce different 'types' of rain, with up to −2/3 stop underexposure in 1/3 stop increments to ensure 'correctly' exposed flowers against the darkish background.

A very straightforward set-up with the tulips neatly arranged and taped to a piece of wood. The mains light is positioned just behind the flowers in the hope of highlighting the 'rain'.

EQUIPMENT

OLYMPUS OM2n

90MM MACRO LENS

TRIPODS

MAINS OPERATED
QUARTZ-IODINE LAMP

BACKGROUND BOARD

STEPS, TULIPS

KODAK ELITE ISO 50 FILM

The 'rain' has registered as long streaks, indicating a longish exposure, yet despite the artificial nature of the rain, the final image is reasonably convincing. I particularly like the splashes (streaks) of water bouncing off the red tulip on the left, which adds a little life to the picture. The drops of water on the flowers and leaves are well lit, underlining the nature of the weather and adding a touch of sparkle to the image. The background is well out of focus and looks more natural than the paint-sprayed background used on some of the other photographs. Exposure: 1/8 sec, f 16, –1/3 stop underexposure. 90mm macro lens. Kodak Elite 50.

The second part of the assignment was to produce an interesting composition of a tulip flower in close-up, filling the entire frame with the petals. I used one of the red tulips some days later when the flower was fully open and almost past its best.

A tiny piece of Plasticine was attached to the front petal to weigh it down and the camera set up with the film plane (camera back) parallel to the main plane of the flower, hoping to keep the most important parts in sharp focus. Strong backlighting was provided by the very bright late afternoon sun and a mirror reflected sunlight onto the front surfaces of the flower, lighting the pistil and stamens. The camera was tripod-mounted and a very small aperture used to produce the maximum depth of field.

This exercise provides plenty of scope for experimentation with the arrangement, the lighting and the 'rain'. For the 'close-up' images the main considerations are effective lighting and good composition.

TIPS

❖ Select complete, undamaged flowers – the others might look fine in a vase, but will not stand up to close scrutiny on a transparency.

❖ Find the most important plane of the flower and set the camera back parallel to it.

❖ When working in close up, use the smallest aperture available to achieve greatest depth of field, even though the central definition may suffer very, very slightly – and always use a substantial tripod and cable release.

HOAR FROST AND ICE

November is noted for its mists, fogs and early frosts and for this assignment I hope to photograph hoar-frost and ice on roses, rose-hips and grasses.

The hoar-frost had developed over several days when the foggy November weather coincided with sub-zero temperatures, allowing ice crystals to gradually build up around the margins of the leaves and petals. On this occasion the early morning fog had lifted as the sun struggled to break through. The rose was almost backlit and, after making several exposures with the camera tripod-mounted, a piece of white card was used to reflect a little light onto the front surfaces of the rose and leaves in case the ambient lighting was insufficient.

The photograph of the rose-hip and autumn leaves was taken on the same day around noon with brilliant sunlight behind the specimen, providing very strong backlighting. As the lens hood seemed to be quite ineffectual, my hand was used to cast a shadow over the lens, hoping it wouldn't appear in the frame. No additional lighting was used in this photograph.

Nature provides the key elements in these images (hoar-frost, ice crystals) but you control the lighting and composition. Experiment with different lighting arrangements and don't be afraid to mix daylight and artificial light, bearing in mind the latter will register yellowish unless a pale blue gel is used.

The flower, leaves and buds are all well positioned in the frame with the leaves at the bottom leading the eye up to the flower. The flower buds are sufficiently subdued in colour not to compete with the red flower. Because the camera back was absolutely parallel to the main plane of the flower and leaves, the image is pin-sharp in all the important areas. The natural background is dark and unobtrusive, forming a solid frame to the picture. Exposure: 1/60 sec, f 11. 90mm macro lens. Kodak Ektachrome 100.

Left: The beauty of this image lies in the contrast between the ice crystals around the margins of the leaves and stems, and the dark, well-out-of-focus background. The composition is little more than adequate, though the horizontal twigs along the bottom edge do form a decent base to the picture. The shadow of my hand on the lens has paid dividends by keeping out the direct rays, resulting in good contrast and detail. Exposure: 1/125 sec, f 11. 90mm macro lens. Kodak Ektachrome 100.

EQUIPMENT

OLYMPUS OM2n

90MM MACRO LENS, TRIPOD

ARTIFICIAL LIGHT SOURCE

WHITE REFLECTOR

KODAK EKTACHROME ISO 100 FILM

This image stands or falls on whether the tone and quality of the backlighting adequately compensates for the general lack of form and colour in the 'weeping' grass. I selected this shot, backlit by the unfiltered car spotlight because the colour is so warm and attractive, almost like a shaft of late evening autumn sunlight.
Each little ice droplet hangs like a jewel, with the whole somewhat resembling a crystal chandelier. I tried to direct most of the light away from the pieces of grass on the right side so as not to detract from the central display. The natural background is well out of focus and non-obtrusive, allowing the iced grass to come to the fore. Exposure: 1/60 sec, f11. 90mm macro lens. Kodak Ektachrome 100.

TIPS

❖ These conditions are somewhat unpredictable quirks of nature and you must be prepared to act quickly.

❖ Search the area because the distribution of hoar-frost can be very patchy, being dependent on shade, shelter and alignment with the moon.

❖ Don't bring your camera directly from the cold outdoors into a warm house or car. Let it warm up slowly in a cooler environment, otherwise the camera, lenses etc. will be covered in condensation, which is bad news for the lens elements and even worse for the camera's electronic circuits.

SPIDER'S WEB

Highlighting the very delicate structure of a spider's web with pin-sharp clarity right across the orb, is the aim of this garden assignment.

Spiders secrete fine silky threads from spinnerets at the end of their abdomens, using it to snare prey and spin cocoons to protect their eggs but most spiders do not spin webs. The large garden spider's orb web is constructed by attaching silken threads to twigs to form a Y-shaped frame. More threads are added like the spokes of a wheel followed by a non-sticky thread spiral working out from the centre. On the return journey the spider eats the first spiral and simultaneously secretes the final sticky spiral thread. An oily substance on the spider's feet prevents it from becoming entangled in its own web.

The best time to photograph spiders' webs is on a misty or foggy autumn morning before the sun has broken through and while the web is still covered with minute water droplets. There were several orb webs available at the bottom of the garden on that particular morning and I searched around to find a near perfect one with the occupant nicely located at the centre. Good access for the camera and tripod and a suitable non-intrusive background are also important.

I first tried photographing a vertical web, realising that to keep it all in sharp focus, the camera would have to point horizontally and include (albeit out of focus) trees, bushes and sky in the background.

Another web, tilted at about 15° to the vertical, allowed me to point the camera down slightly to include an acceptable background. A range of lighting was used starting with daylight only, followed by flash to backlight the web. Finally a small video light was held at varying distances behind and above the web, again providing a backlight. Several exposures were made at f16 (aperture priority) bracketed down to −1 stop, on Ektachrome 64 set at ISO 80, with the camera tripod-mounted and the shutter triggered using a cable release.

As the gossamer threads were so fine and delicate, the slightest air current caused them to sway in and out of focus, exacerbated by the longish 1/4 sec exposure. If the web is drying out, very fine water droplets can be sprayed on, courtesy of a house plant mist sprayer. Direct the mist well above the web, allowing the droplets to float down into it; direct spraying will damage the web.

This is an earlier shot of an almost vertical web. The composition is interesting with the dead stem and flower stalks of the hogweed helping to frame the picture while the spider is positioned at one of the strong points where the thirds intersect. The background includes trees and sky, which register as a radially symmetrical, out-of-focus pattern, with splashes of light radiating from behind the centre of the web. An interesting background but rather too distracting. Exposure: 1/4sec, f 16. 90mm macro lens. Kodak Ektachrome 64.

EQUIPMENT

OLYMPUS OM2n

90MM MACRO LENS

T32 FLASH UNIT

SMALL VIDEO LIGHT

TRIPOD, CABLE RELEASE

EKTACHROME 64 FILM

A good example of radial symmetry with the spider in the centre but quite low in the frame. The dry hogweed stem indicates that the upper dead flower stalks are supporting the web. The water droplets are highlighted using the small video light held approximately 25cm (10 in) above and behind the web. Even at f16 the background is well out of focus, registering as an attractive, non-intrusive combination of dark browns and greens. (The shots taken without the video light were very flat with the web barely visible, while the flash shots resulted in a black background). Exposure: 1/4 sec, f 16, –2/3 stop underexposure. 90mm macro lens. Kodak Ektachrome 64.

TIPS

❖ Ideal weather conditions – misty morning and no wind.

❖ Search for undamaged web complete with spider, with good camera access and empty space behind it.

❖ Set up camera back absolutely parallel to the web and select a small aperture (f 11–16) to ensure the whole web is in sharp focus. Use the preview lever (or button) to check that the background is well out of focus.

❖ A hand-held video light is useful to highlight the water droplets.

GARDEN BIRDS IN WINTER

In this assignment we are hoping to produce pin-sharp close-up images of a range of garden birds.

Birds are desperate for food during the cold winter months and should be fed regularly every day. The food should be energy-rich and nutritious and could include, in addition to soaked bread and table scraps, peanuts, proprietary mixed wildbird seed, pieces of apple and pear, earthworms and mealworms. Another method of obtaining a food supply is to collect seeds, berries, nuts and fruit in the autumn and store them for winter use.

Birds must have a regular supply of water and, although many die of starvation during a severe winter, without water they will die much sooner.

An obvious starting point is to set up a bird table liberally supplied with mixed wildbird seed, plus a hanging container of peanuts. The former will attract all the seed eating birds including sparrows, blackbirds, starlings, chaffinches, greenfinches, yellowhammers and pigeons. A robin will occasionally partake but he prefers something live and wriggling such as earthworms, maggots and mealworms. The hanging peanut container is a magnet for all the tit family and the occasional woodpecker, but when you want to do some bird photography look for something more natural, such as an old tree stump or a pine log complete with bark. Food, including mixed seeds and ground up peanuts, is placed on the top of the tree stump but discreetly hidden from the camera lens, while the pine log, set up vertically, has a few 15mm holes drilled in it, filled with suet and ground peanuts – again out of view of the camera lens.

To conceal you from the birds and to get sufficiently close to obtain a decent-sized image you will need a hide. I work from the far end of my garage behind a wooden door which opens on to the garden. Two holes, one for the camera lens and the other for easy viewing, were cut about one metre high so that I can sit observing the bird activity. (If you are considering using a living room or extension, the windows facing the garden should be covered to conceal you from the birds.)

Bird photographs can be taken using daylight only but as the light levels in winter are usually low and unpredictable, I much prefer to use electronic flash because of its high light intensity and short flash duration (usually 1/1000 sec or less). It is reliable and excellent photographs can be taken on the dullest days. The main light (one or two flash units) was set at 45° to the side and above the subject at a distance of approximately 1.5 metres.

EQUIPMENT

OLYMPUS OM2n

75–300 SIGMA ZOOM LENS,
500MM SIGMA TELEPHOTO LENS

SEVERAL FLASH UNITS INCLUDING 2
METZ 45CL3S AND 3 OLYMPUS T32S

MATERIALS AND BACKGROUND
BOARDS FOR THE SET-UP

TRIPOD, CABLE RELEASE

KODAK ELITE II ISO 100 FILM.

Having seen the female great spotted woodpecker, Dencrocopos major, only twice, I decided to include the shot, even though the peanut holder looks a little incongruous. Despite working from a fixed position with a 500mm lens, the quite large bird fits reasonably well into the frame. The woodpecker's head is well positioned at the intersection of thirds and, although the eye surround is well lit, the eye itself is quite black and lacking a highlight. The background colours are in keeping with the scene and unobtrusive, but are possibly a little too light.
Exposure: multiple flash, f 16,
–2/3 stop compensation. 500mm lens.
Kodak Elite 100.

The robin, Erithacus rubecula, was one of
several shots taken during the birds' frequent
visits to the maggots which I put down
regularly. The composition is satisfactory
with more space in front of the robin's head
than behind, allowing the robin to look into
the picture towards the viewer. The all-
important eye is in sharp focus but the twin
catchlights indicate a two-flash main-light
arrangement. The robin is standing up to its
full height, looking quite pleased with itself.
There is just a hint of backlighting which
lifts the robin away from the dark, out-of-
focus background, while the sloping
foreground adds some interest to the
composition. Exposure: multiple flash,
f 16, −1 stop compensation. 500mm lens.
Kodak Elite 50.

A fill-in flash was positioned at the other side level with the subject and the same distance away. Finally a fairly high backlight was used to help separate the subject from the background. The flashes didn't seem to affect the birds adversely because they returned time after time to the feeding point. I could afford the luxury of stopping down the lens to f 16–f 22 and still have a flash duration of around 1/1000 sec or less but the focal plane shutter with its flash synch of only 1/60 sec is obviously not sufficiently short to prevent the occasional secondary ghost image on the transparency.

If a natural background is within 1–2 metres of the subject you can probably use it, but anything further away will register black in the final image. I prefer to use a suitably coloured background board set up about 1–2 metres behind the subject.

The other alternative is to move the background board well back (up to 3 metres) and light it independently using a separate flash unit. After making several test exposures with the board at different distances, a board-to-flash distance of 1 metre resulted in a correctly exposed background.

I worked from inside the garage using a 75–300mm zoom lens or a 500mm telephoto lens attached to the Olympus SLR camera. During a morning and afternoon session totalling around five hours, at least one film was exposed which was processed locally within the hour. After examining the transparencies, any changes to the lighting or the exposure could be made before more film was exposed the following day. The photographs were taken over a period of weeks between early December and late February.

This is a very absorbing long-term project well within the competence of any nature photographer. With time and plenty of patience you should be able to capture many appealing images.

The long-tailed tit, Aegithalos caudatus, is well positioned in the frame with the long, tilted-up tail just clearing the edge of the frame. Due to the black feathers around the head, the eye (also black) is hardly discernible and lacks a catchlight. The rotting stump forms a suitable base to the picture while the background, is non-distracting and therefore satisfactory. Exposure: multiple flash, f 16, −1 stop compensation. 500mm lens. Kodak Elite 50.

Inquisitive dunnock, Prunella modularis, looking for food. Being side-on to the camera, the beak, head and breast are all pin-sharp with a well-defined, rusty-orange eye complete with catchlight. The greenery on the left is partially balanced by the sloping timber on the right with the well out-of-focus green background completing the picture. Exposure: multiple flash, f 22, −2/3 stop compensation. 500mm lens. Kodak Elite 50.

Above: In this portrait of a female blackbird, Turdus merula, I particularly liked the rich brown colours in the feathers, and the symmetry and fine detail in both the breast plumage and the fan-shaped spread of feathers just below the eye. The bird looks alert and perky with a useful catchlight (or two!) in the eye. This fine portrait is somewhat diminished by the rather bland background. Exposure: multiple flash, f 16, −2/3 stop compensation. 500mm lens. Kodak Elite 50.

The blue tit, Parus caeruleus, nature's little acrobat, distracted for a split second by some wriggling maggots just below. It is well positioned and nicely framed by the pine trunk, side branches and green needles. Exposure: multiple flash, f 22, −2/3 stop compensation. 500mm lens. Kodak Elite 50.

TIPS

❖ Birds will always visit your garden if the right type of food is put out regularly for them.

❖ Bird tables and peanut holders are fine for regular feeding but use something more natural for your bird photography.

❖ Ensure that the food is out of view of the camera by putting it in depressions or in holes drilled in the side of the log or branch.

❖ Birds are very active with very quick head movements, making short duration flash lighting a useful tool.

Grey Squirrel in Winter

In this garden workshop we hope to produce a pin-sharp portrait of a grey squirrel, tail held high, eating nuts.

The grey squirrel's natural habitat is woodland where its main source of food is nuts, foliage and the various fruits and seeds of deciduous trees.

Photograph squirrels in the winter when their natural food is in short supply because they will then come regularly to the garden if you put out daily supplies of hazelnuts, sweet chestnuts or peanuts. Like most mammals they tend to be lazy, making a readily available meal preferable to having to search for it.

I used the garage as a hide, having cut two holes in the side door approximately 10 cm and 16 cm in diameter, 120 cm above ground level so that I could sit fairly comfortably for several hours. The camera was mounted on a very substantial tripod with the lens behind the larger hole while I used the other to keep an eye on the activity in the garden.

A piece of tree stump which had a natural flat top surface with a depression in it to conceal the food supply was arranged about 2.5 metres from the camera. Although it is quite possible to take squirrel photographs using available light, several factors militate against this. The light level in the winter is often quite low requiring a large lens aperture, fast film or long exposures. A large aperture results in a shallow depth of field with much of the animal out of focus, while a fast film (e.g. ISO 400) is not conducive to recording the fine detail in the fur and whiskers. Long exposures (e.g. 1/4 sec) will not arrest subject movement and a blurred head or forelimb is not acceptable.

The flash units were arranged with a main light positioned 45° above and 45° to the side, with a fill-in light on the other side level with the subject's head. A light was also placed above and behind as a backlight to help separate the subject from the background.

In many gardens the natural background (a hedge) might well be several metres behind the subject and, if the latter is correctly exposed, the background will register completely black. It could be specially lit by another flash unit but a few experimental exposures would be required to find the best flash-to-background distance.

I prefer to use an artificial background and have one or two boards approximately 90 x 120 cm (35 x 47 in) sprayed in various shades of green and brown to look as natural as possible. The selected board was propped up, about 1.5 metres behind the subject and, to ensure that no tell-tale shadows of twigs or cables were cast on the background, a powerful torch was shone from the position of each flash unit.

Settling down on a chair in the garage with the camera roughly focused, I observed the activity through the viewing hole in the door. When a squirrel approached, the camera was fine focused and the exposure made. This sounds easy, but often the squirrel would sit with its back to the camera, eat all the food and disappear, while on other occasions its tail was in the 'down' position or its stance ungainly.

This is an easy assignment where excellent close-up images can be captured using a medium focal length zoom lens of modest aperture. Flash will 'freeze' any movement and allow you to use a small aperture for increased depth of field.

EQUIPMENT

OLYMPUS OM2n

70–300MM TELEPHOTO LENS

TRIPOD, THREE T32 FLASH UNITS

BACKGROUND BOARD

PLANT MATERIAL (FOR THE SET)
AND PLENTY OF FOOD
(FOR THE SQUIRRELS)

KODAK ELITE 100 FILM.

Above: I think this shot works even though the squirrel is not in the classical pose, is not feeding, and has its tail down and out of the frame. The composition is satisfactory, with the tree stump at the bottom left balancing the dark green foliage at the top right, both helping to frame the picture. The squirrel's head and eye are situated at a strong point in the frame, while the catchlight in the eye adds a little life to what would otherwise be a rather lifeless black mass. Despite its good points, the picture might be criticised because the background is almost black, while the evergreen leaves are slightly too obtrusive, pulling the viewer's eye away from the squirrel. Exposure: multiple flash, f 16. 200mm lens. Kodak Elite 100.

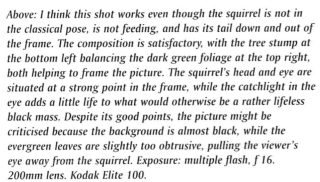

TIPS

❖ Squirrels are lazy and will visit your garden for a 'ready-made' meal.

❖ They keep their heads down while feeding but any noise (generated by you) will cause them to look up – be ready to take the photograph.

❖ To obtain the classic shot of a squirrel sitting upright, looking at the camera and with its tail up, requires time and patience. Fortunately squirrels return at very regular intervals to the feeding site.

This shot, showing the squirrel in a classical pose with its bushy tale held high and nibbling a nut, was one of half a dozen or so taken one cold January afternoon. The composition is fairly straightforward with the squirrel standing on a tree stump and looking to the left to meet the viewer's eyes as they scan the picture. The squirrel is nicely framed with the tree stump acting as a solid base and the evergreen leaves forming the top of the frame, while the out-of-focus background is in dark, harmonising colours. Exposure: multiple flash, f 16. 200mm lens. Kodak Elite 100.

HEDGEHOG

The aim of this assignment is to produce some appealing close-up images of the common hedgehog in its natural environment.

Being mainly nocturnal, the hedgehog emerges at dusk and hunts throughout the night, feeding on insect larvae, worms, frogs, mice and the eggs of ground-nesting birds. It also eats acorns, berries and household scraps; the latter being much better than the traditional bread and milk which, if provided regularly, tend to give the hedgehog diarrhoea.

The hedgehog's eyesight is poor, but its senses of smell and hearing are acute, enabling it to operate in the dark and locate its food quite easily. It is also a good runner, swimmer and climber, having been found high up trees, drainpipes and rough creeper-clad walls.

While photographing a fox in the back garden at night, I noticed up to three hedgehogs feeding on the nuts, wildbird seed and chicken pieces put out for the birds and fox. Although the hedgehog is quite a fast mover, a light touch with my foot caused it to roll up into a ball and remain completely still. Tough gardening gloves were worn (the spines are needle-sharp and often infected) to transfer it to the garden shed, along with some food, water and dry grass bedding.

The following morning the curled up hedgehog was placed on a raised (25 cm, 10 in) part of the rockery, setting the camera, complete with macro lens and extension tube, as low as possible to obtain an almost ground level view of the hedgehog. The Metz 45 flash unit was hand-held about 30cm (12 in) away at an angle of approximately 30° to the horizontal, hoping to illuminate the dark, well-concealed eyes. A few freshly dug worms were placed close by.

After about half a minute, the hedgehog began to uncurl, looked around, then very quickly scuttled off to a narrow gap between a nearby wall and a drainpipe. No time to focus, let alone take a photograph. I repositioned it and waited again for it to uncurl and show its head, managing only one exposure before it scampered off again to the shelter of the drainpipe. The whole process was repeated three or four times. On the last occasion the hedgehog inadvertently rolled onto its back, relaxed its abdominal muscles and slowly uncurled. Three photographs were taken of the uncurling process, after which the hedgehog was returned to the hedge bottom from which it emerged each evening.

EQUIPMENT

BRONICA ETRSi MEDIUM FORMAT
(6 X 4.5 CM) SLR CAMERA

100MM MACRO LENS

E-28 EXTENSION TUBE

CLOSE-UP LENS, BENBO TRIPOD

METZ 45 ELECTRONIC FLASH UNIT

VELVIA ISO 50 FILM.

This was the only shot of the hedgehog in full side view with the head extended and the eye clearly visible. Because the film plane was parallel to the hedgehog's side, the definition from the tip of the nose to the rear end is very sharp. The extended head shows the conical muzzle, the position of the ears and the location of the coarse hairs, while the eye is well defined with a life-enhancing catchlight clearly visible.

The green and brown background harmonises with the browns in the hedgehog, although the greenery might be considered too bright and too well defined and therefore somewhat distracting.
Exposure: flash and daylight, f 16. 100mm macro lens. Extension tube. Fuji Velvia.

TIPS

❖ Always wear stout gardening gloves when handling hedgehogs as they are carriers of disease.

❖ To stop a scuttling hedgehog in its tracks, gently touch it with a stick or your foot, when it will 'freeze' immediately, rolling up into a tight ball.

❖ Supplying small earthworms will keep the hedgehog 'happy' during a photo session.

❖ Photography at ground level will provide a more interesting image than one taken from above, looking down.

Red Fox at Night

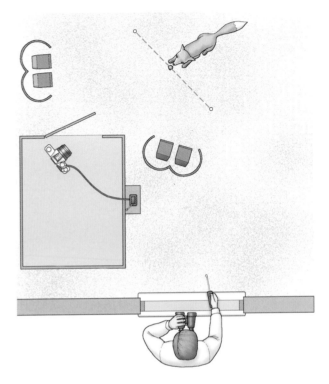

Photographing a wild urban fox was never going to be easy, but that is the aim of this long-duration night-time assignment.

A few of the assignments described in this book were completed in half a day, while others dragged on for several months before any acceptable photographs were secured. Photographing the red fox came into the latter category.

It all started some five months earlier in June, when my wife who, with great regularity, feeds the garden birds, squirrels and hedgehogs, noticed the occasional passage of a fox across the bottom of our long garden. Not one to miss an opportunity of observing and enjoying more wildlife, out went a chicken wing and drumstick every evening at dusk.

Gradually a routine was established and the fox (occasionally a dog and a vixen) would appear some 10–50 minutes after the food had been put out.

I waited until the routine was fairly well established and in late July decided to make a start on the photography. The camera was set up in the garden shed at right angles to, and 6 metres from, an imaginary line 3 metres long, with a white marker (small plastic bottle) at either end. The camera was focused on a 'fox-sized' box placed in the centre of the line, adjusting the zoom lens so that the markers were just out of frame.

Flash lighting was provided by two Metz 45s secured 2.5 metres up a flowering cherry tree, 4 metres from the centre of the line. Another pair of flash units providing some frontal lighting, were attached to the side of the shed; 2 metres high and 6 metres from the line. Finally the food was placed in the centre of the line with the camera already pre-focused on it.

This was the final arrangement; earlier flash positions must have been too close to the food as the fox was extremely cautious and wouldn't come sufficiently close to snatch its evening meal. Thinking that the high-pitched (ultrasonic) whistle from the flash units might be unnerving the fox, each unit was covered with an insulating jacket made from thick carpet underfelt, which not only deadened the sound, but kept the Ni Cad. batteries warm. In wet weather, the flash units were protected using transparent polythene freezer bags.

After several unsuccessful attempts, I wondered whether sitting in the shed with the door partially open was alarming the fox, so removed myself completely, operating the camera and flash units from an upstairs bedroom some 30 metres away using a short range radio remote control unit (maximum range 40 metres, response time 0.2 seconds).

Equipment

OLYMPUS OM2n SLR

75–300MM ZOOM LENS

FOUR METZ 45 FLASH UNITS

BENBO TRIPOD

SHORT RANGE RADIO REMOTE CONTROL UNIT

FUJI SENSIA ISO 200 AND 400.

The fox was always very wary when approaching the food, often coming within a metre or so and then, for some unknown (to me) reason, backing off and slowly circling the area before cautiously approaching the food again. We usually put out two pieces of uncooked chicken (wing and drumstick), hoping that the fox would come twice giving two opportunities for taking photographs. This rarely happened as the fox invariably picked up both pieces in one fast swoop. The fox is on the imaginary line, well positioned in the frame and in sharp focus. The black background gives the correct impression that the photograph was taken with flash on a dark night around 10 p.m. Exposure: multiple flash, f 8, –1 stop underexposure. 75–300mm zoom lens. Fuji Sensia 200.

From this high vantage point and with the help of a pair of 7 x 50 binoculars (which provided a useful level of night vision), I could just about see when the fox was inside the markers and on the imaginary line and therefore hopefully in focus. Typically two to three hours would be spent in the darkened bedroom, peering through the binoculars looking for the silent, shadowy fox, making one, or on a 'good' night two, exposures, although on many occasions I came away with nothing more than eyestrain and a splitting headache. Trying to photograph the fox continued intermittently until early November when I decided to call it a day.

If you are looking for an interesting project, this could be it, but doing it this way is time consuming, albeit very absorbing. Why not try photographing young fox cubs near their 'earth' (local gamekeepers can often point you in the right direction) as they are much less wary of humans.

For this shot the zoom lens was set to produce a slightly larger image of the fox, which is well positioned in the frame, with the food already in its jaws as it makes for a gap in the hedge. Being right on the pre-focused line, the fox is sharply focused while the very short flash duration has 'frozen' the fox's movement quite well. This represents the best shot after several weeks of intermittent night work. Exposure: multiple flash, f 8, –1 stop underexposure. 75–300mm zoom lens. Fuji Sensia 200. (See page 12 for another 'fox at night' shot.)

TIPS

❖ If possible work with someone who is already feeding foxes – it could save you an awful lot of time.

❖ Foxes' sense of smell (and sight) is very well developed – handle the food with gloves and distance yourself from the food point.
Some method of remote firing of the camera and flash units is desirable.

❖ Listed guide numbers for flash units do not apply out of doors where there are few reflecting surfaces. Actual guide number is less than half, therefore you require a lot of flash power, particularly if the units are several metres away from the subject.
I use four Metz 45s.

CHAPTER TEN

Studio Workshop

Wildlife photography is by its very nature an outdoor pursuit, but when the weather is too wretched to take photographs I occasionally visit a local tropical house to photograph exotic plants and animals from the hot, steamy regions of the world. During the winter months there are few visitors, allowing photographic work to proceed undisturbed.

The warm, humid atmosphere in the tropical house can soon mist up cold lenses and camera eye-pieces and as a precaution carry your equipment on the car floor next to a heater outlet and carry it as quickly as possible, in an insulated holdall, into the tropical house. Photography through the glass sides of an aquarium or reptile enclosure is not difficult if you keep the camera lens parallel to and almost touching the glass, when the latter acts as a plane glass filter, allowing the camera to 'penetrate' the aquarium or reptile enclosure. As with any filter, the glass must be absolutely clean and free from in-built blemishes or scratches. The light level in tropical houses is often quite low making flash mandatory and if you tilt the flash unit down very slightly, there will be less chance of any reflection from the back wall of the enclosure registering as an ugly hot spot on the transparency.

A lot of my nature photography is done at home, in what I euphemistically call my 'studio', which is, in reality, the floored-out, partially glazed loft. It is a 13 x 20 ft (3.9 x 6.1 m) multi-purpose room used as a photographic darkroom and as a storage space. But its main use is for photographing small plants, flowers and animals in close-up, using a 39 x 20 in (100 x 51 cm) table placed firmly in the centre of the floor to build sets on, do pond-life microscopy and to support the flight tunnel used to photograph insects flying and frogs leaping.

The advantages of working in the loft are numerous: a temperature-controlled environment (well, almost!), no wind or rain, no interruptions, and hot liquid refreshments available at the flick of a switch. For work which requires careful, accurate handling of animals, plants and equipment, this environment is ideal and sets can be left undisturbed for hours or even days. You could use a study, kitchen or conservatory, in fact anywhere where you can work undisturbed and where the light level is reasonably high.

The cotton-topped tamarin, Saguinus oedipus oedipus, lives in the northern Colombian forests, where numbers have decreased to a dangerously low level. Captive breeding programmes are the only way to increase their numbers again. Photograph taken in a tropical house through glass with the flash unit on top of the camera, which was hand-held and manually focused. Exposure: flash, f11, –2/3 stop underexposure. 90mm macro lens. Kodak Elite 100.

The gerbil (photographed in an empty aquarium) standing on its hind legs, was more difficult to photograph as it is unstable and remains in this position for less than a second at any time. However it is reasonably well framed and the head and eye are the first parts noticed by the viewer as he scans the picture from the top left side. The black background certainly makes the gerbil stand out well but it may be too oppressive and doesn't seem to impart any impression of depth. Exposure: flash, f11, -1 stop compensation. 90mm macro lens. Ektachrome 100.

Above: The two tree frogs taking a photo-call in the flight tunnel prior to performing their leaping act! All the digits are firmly clasped around the twig, with the sucker tips clearly visible. Note the loose, supple skin across the 'chest' between the front legs of the lower frog and the reticular nature of the skin above and below. The under-chin region of the upper frog is inflated as part of the breathing process (frogs have only tiny lungs and no ribcage). Exposure: multiple flash, f16. 75mm lens. Kodak Ektachrome 64.

Right: American green tree-frog, Hyla cinerea, photographed in the 'studio', using two flash units, a main one above and a fill-in to one side.

TIPS

❖ Always get as close as possible to the glass, using a finger end wedged between the camera lens and the glass to act as a shock absorber for the camera and the frog

❖ The glass must be scrupulously clean – use window-cleaning fluid if necessary, but obtain permission first.

❖ Move the flash unit off the camera lens optical axis to prevent possible reflections of the flash from the rear wall of the enclosure showing up on the film.

COMMON FROG

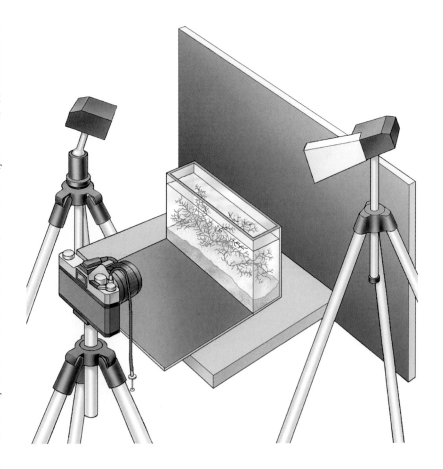

I n late March a couple of frogs were collected and taken home to an already set-up and stabilised aquarium. This was home-made using pieces of window glass bonded together with clear silicone sealer-adhesive. It measures 30 x 20 x 7 cm (12 x 8 x 2.5in), the small dimension being the front-to-back distance. This limits the movement of the frog making photography that much easier.

Small pebbles, boiled in water to kill any algae and bacteria, which would soon foul and cloud the water, were placed in the bottom of the empty aquarium. Pieces of pondweed were tied with cotton to pebbles, after which filtered pond water was gently poured in and the whole set-up left for 24 hours to settle and stabilise.

A pair of T32 flash units provided the lighting, one in the 45° frontal position, about 30 cm away and towards one end of the aquarium. The other provided high backlighting, the same distance away and near to the other end. The latter was fitted with a piece of card on the nearside to prevent the flash striking the camera lens. To provide a dark, non-obtrusive background a piece of black velvet was positioned some 50 cm (20 in) behind the aquarium and, to eliminate possible reflections, the aquarium was stood on a large piece of matt black card.To prevent reflections of the camera and myself in the front glass of the aquarium, I fitted a piece of black cardboard, 38 x 28 cm (15 x 11 in) with a hole cut in the centre, onto the end of the lens barrel. Finally the frogs were carefully lowered into the water and allowed to settle down. After a couple of hours of photography the frogs were returned to their pond where they quickly disappeared to the bottom.

This is a straightforward assignment well within the competency of any nature photographer, but remember that moving frogs will disturb the water releasing small, but distracting, pieces of plant weed. Give them time to settle down before starting your photography.

EQUIPMENT

OLYMPUS OM2n

90MM MACRO LENS

AQUARIUM

TRIPOD

TWO OLYMPUS T32 FLASH UNITS

KODAK ELITE 50 FILM

Above: The arrangement is fairly straightforward with the pebbles forming a 'solid', sloping base to the picture while the upper two-thirds is filled with attractive pondweed and a cluster of frog-spawn, all against a black, non-reflecting background.

Right: I like this shot because it suggests movement, with the frog leaning to the left in a state of dynamic imbalance. It is pushing its way through the water plants up to the surface probably to take in air. The pebbles form a solid base to the picture in contrast to the swaying stems of the plants, while frog-spawn at the top left catches the eye, leading it down towards the main centre of interest – the frog's head. As in all animal photographs, the eye(s) must be clearly visible, in sharp focus and where possible showing a catchlight. Exposure: flash, f 16, –2/3 stop compensation. 90mm macro lens. Kodak Elite 50.

TIPS

❖ Care of the front glass – no greasy marks or in-built blemishes.

❖ Frogs move around a lot disturbing the water and the pondweeds – filter the former and carefully wash the latter.

❖ Frogs' eyes are a very prominent feature – must always be pin-sharp and with a catchlight if possible.

SMOOTH NEWT

The aim of this workshop is to produce some appealing images of smooth newts as they go about their normal activities in the confines of a small aquarium.

For most people the mention of a newt conjures up an image of a very small, long-tailed, four-legged creature swimming around in a pond. In reality the newt (like the frog) is a terrestrial animal spending most of its life in damp habitats including wet heathland, bogs, marshes and damp pastures. However, (again like the frog) it must return to the pond in the breeding season.

As newts are now a rare species, I was fortunate to obtain four or five from a newt enthusiast who has several breeding ponds in his garden. In a good season he is able to release many small newts back into local ponds in an effort to re-establish them.

The newts were collected with some pond water and kept outside overnight when the cool temperature slowed them down. They can then be handled quite easily with cold hands (hold your hands under the cold tap for a minute or two).

The same set-up was used which had served me so well for the frog photography, i.e. small aquarium, two flash units etc. During the photo session I noticed one of the newts clasping some pondweed in preparation for egg laying. This was not too difficult to photograph as the newt was too preoccupied with the business of laying eggs to worry about me or the camera.

Finally some action shots were taken by following the newts around the aquarium with the camera pre-focused and supported on a monopod. The latter not only provided some stability but also allowed me to rock the camera back and forth to keep the newt in sharp focus.

EQUIPMENT

OLYMPUS OM2n

90MM MACRO LENS

SMALL AQUARIUM

MATT-BLACK-FACED CARD

BLACK VELVET BACKGROUND

TWO T32 FLASH UNITS

A female smooth newt in a delightfully graceful pose as she swims to the surface, while a male sits at the bottom staring at the camera. Getting two newts in focus requires patience and not a little luck and in this shot the head and eyes of both newts are sharply defined. On the negative side, the pebbles are too bright and a reflection of the female is just discernible in the rear glass of the aquarium. Although the newts' heads are well located at the 'intersection of thirds', this may split the interest and detract from the overall composition. Exposure: flash, f 11, −2/3 stop. 2 x T32 flash units. Kodak Elite 50.

Above: In the breeding season the male smooth newt develops a dorsal crest, a yellow-orange belly and a silver-blue tail stripe. The diagonal positioning in the frame and the sinuous tail suggest movement, as the newt makes its way to the surface. The pondweed behind it is, fortunately, slightly out of focus, while the newt's head is highlighted against the black background, helped by the rear flash unit which has put a just discernible rim of light around the head. Exposure: flash, f 16, −2/3 stop. 2 x T32 flash units. Kodak Elite 50.

Right: A female smooth newt clasping some pondweed with its rear legs, during the egg-laying process. The newt is well positioned in the frame and, by keeping the film plane (camera back) parallel to it, her entire body from the tip of the nose to the end of the tail is in sharp focus. The dark, underlit pebbles form a solid foundation to the picture and the slightly 'soft' weed behind the newt adds an attractive harmonising colour. Criticisms might be that there are no eggs visible, while an unidentified double streak to the left and a piece of dangling white plant stem on the right are distractions. Exposure: flash, f 16, −2/3 stop. 2 x T32 flash units. Kodak Elite 50.

TIPS

❖ The tips on the frog apply equally to newt photography.

❖ Newts are easy to handle if kept in cold water and handled with cold hands.

❖ If photographing two newts together, head and eyes of both (not just one) must be in sharp focus.

THE RAMSHORN SNAIL

Left undisturbed, the tiny ramshorn snail will pull itself away from the shell and begin to feed. This is what we hope to capture on film in this indoor workshop.

Pond snails can easily be picked out of the pond by hand, whereas a net is used to catch the fast-moving beetles, sticklebacks and newts. A small, fine-meshed fishing net is quite adequate for this purpose. A liberal supply of various pondweeds should also be collected using hooked wire attached to the end of a long cane. Placing a white 12 x 10 in developing tray (or a piece of opaque plastic sheeting) on the grass, all the material was emptied into it. Some of the pond creatures were picked up by hand and placed in a jam jar while the small ones were removed using a small pipette (or medicine dropper) or small spoon and placed in a specimen tube. Some plants and filamentous algae were selected, after which all unwanted material was returned to the pond.

Before leaving the pond I collected several litres of pond water, which is preferable to tap water although the latter can be used for topping-up if it has been allowed to stand for 24 hours to dechlorinate. Back at home, the pondweed and the non-predaceous creatures (pond snails, caddis larvae etc.) were transferred into a large aquarium and given time to settle down.

To photograph the ramshorn snail, a tiny aquarium or cell was prepared using two pieces of thin plane glass approximately 12.5 x 10 cm (5 x 4 in), separated by a short length of clear plastic tubing flexed into a U-shape, all held together with two strong rubber bands (cells of various 'thicknesses' can be made using different diameter tubing). After two-thirds filling the cell with filtered pond water, I carefully washed some pieces of pondweed and put them together with several ramshorn snails into the cell.

Because the snail shells are almost transparent, a well-shielded T32 flash unit was used as a strong backlight. It was placed about 20 cm (8 in) above and slightly behind the cell while much weaker frontal lighting was provided by another T32 flash unit positioned at cell height about 40 cm (16 in) in front and diffused with a white handkerchief.

To obtain a decently large image of the tiny 5mm diameter snail shell, the 50mm macro lens was reversed onto a bellows unit supported on a tripod. To increase the contrast between the snail

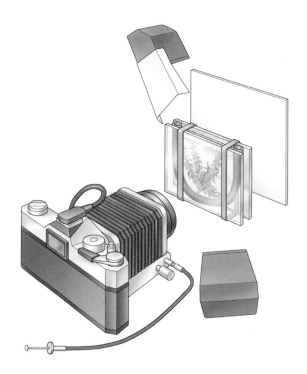

and the background, a piece of black velvet was positioned some 20 cm (8 in) behind the cell.

To prevent reflections of the camera and my head in the front glass of the cell, I attached a 25 x 20 cm (10 x 8 in) piece of matt black card, with a hole cut in the centre, to the lens barrel. Finally the camera was set up parallel to the front glass, which must be scrupulously clean and free from scratches or in-built manufacturing blemishes.

The ISO 50 film was set at 64 with exposures reduced by 1 stop to prevent the strong backlighting washing out the image of the shell and to keep the background really black. A set aperture of f 11 resulted in a working or effective aperture of around f 32, taking into account the bellows extension. Aperture priority and TTL flash were used.

A straightforward assignment requiring careful handling of the equipment and the pond snails, bearing in mind that at magnifications of life-size and beyond, the depth of field is very small indeed, calling for critical focusing, well stopped-down lens, and powerful flash lighting.

EQUIPMENT

OLYMPUS OM2n CAMERA

50MM MACRO LENS

BELLOWS UNIT

TWO FLASH UNITS

MINIATURE AQUARIUM

COLLECTING EQUIPMENT.

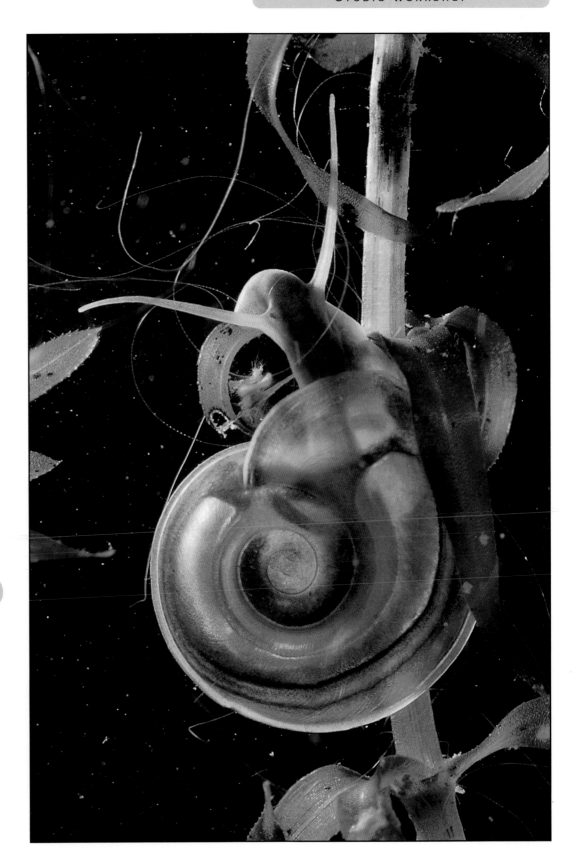

The snail is well positioned with pieces of pondweed framing it at various points. The head and tentacles are clearly defined and well lit with a small, ill-defined eye just visible at the base of each tentacle. The black background has registered well and is in striking contrast to the light tones of the snail and shell yet, despite filtering the water, distracting particles of debris and fine strands of algae are clearly visible and highlighted by the strong backlighting. Exposure: flash, f 32, 1 stop underexposure. Reversed 50mm macro lens. Kodak Ektachrome 50.

TIPS

❖ The glass in the miniature aquarium must be free from scratches and blemishes – greasy marks will be very conspicuous in the final picture.

❖ Filter the pond water through fine nylon as tiny specks will be horribly obvious when backlit.

❖ The black card pushed onto the lens barrel is vital, but when working very close, reflections of the lens manufacturer's name and number can also appear in the glass – use a ring of black cartridge paper to cover them up.

WATER BOATMAN

The aim of this indoor workshop is to produce well-composed close-ups of a water boatman in its natural environment.

The water boatman, Notonecta glauca, is, rather surprisingly, an insect with two pairs of wings and the ability to fly yet it spends virtually all its life in water, flying only very occasionally from pond to pond. In common with all insects it has three pairs of legs, two compound eyes and a pair of small (but hidden) antennae.

Water boatman live underwater, occasionally floating up to the surface, tail-end first, to take in a supply of air. A notable feature is their ability to swim upside down, using their powerful, well-developed third pair of legs as oars; the whole effect resembling a tiny boat being rowed along (hence the popular name).

The set-up was the same as that used for the ramshorn snail photographs with one T32 flash unit in the 45° frontal position and the other high up behind the miniature aquarium to provide some backlighting. Exposures were made at f 22 with −1 stop compensation to ensure a correctly exposed subject and background.

This is a fairly straightforward exercise in close-up photography using living material. The boatman will often remain completely still for several minutes, allowing plenty of time to position it accurately in the frame and achieve good composition.

EQUIPMENT

OLYMPUS OM2n

50MM MACRO LENS

BELLOWS UNIT

TWO FLASH UNITS

MINIATURE AQUARIUM

KODAK EKTACHROME 50.

The water boatman, held by surface tension on the underside of the water film, has come to the surface for air. The head, eyes and three pairs of legs are all in sharp focus with the third pair symmetrically positioned in the frame. The underside of the water surface is acting like a mirror, producing a sharp, albeit foreshortened, image of the underside of the bug with the long third pair of legs clearly visible. Exposure: flash, f 22, −1 stop underexposure. Kodak Ektachrome 50.

The water boatman is searching among the plants for small invertebrates for its next meal. The lighting is similar to that used in previous photographs but the main flash is now more frontal, lighting the side of the body and legs, while the backlight has grazed the horny wing, highlighting its surface texture. The diagonal position of the boatman adds a sense of movement, while the all-important head and eyes are located at a strong point where the imaginary lines dividing the frame into thirds intersect. The plant stem on the left assists in the framing with the almost black background helping to bring forward the water boatman and the plants, resulting in an almost three-dimensional effect. Despite using filtered water, fine particulate matter and strands of filamentous algae are a visual distraction. Exposure: flash, f 22, –1 stop underexposure. Kodak Ektachrome 50.

TIPS

❖ Refer back to the tips on the ramshorn snail.

❖ Keep the large compound eyes in sharp focus.

❖ Third pair of legs are very long – easy to chop off the ends inadvertently.

WATER FLEA

I n this workshop assignment we are hoping to produce some attractive and unusual images of a water flea, using a range of lighting techniques.

Sorting through the pondweeds and water, I noticed several water fleas swimming around and, although they are only pinhead size, their very jerky swimming movement gives them away. One was carefully transferred with a drop of water, to a cavity slide protected by a cover slip, and placed on the microscope stage. After attaching the Olympus camera body to the microscope via an adapter tube, the Metz 45 flash unit was accurately aligned, pointing horizontally at the half-silvered mirror located at the base of the microscope.

The image of the Daphnia was focused on a special focusing screen with a very fine matt surface and a clear cross-hairs centre, using the microscope's own built-in lighting system. I could have taken photographs using this set-up (i.e. without flash) but the exposures would have been quite long (not ideal for living material) and the colour temperature way out. By using flash the exposure was probably less than 1/1000 sec with the colour temperature matching that of the film. Exposures were bracketed between +1 and +2 stops in 1/3 stop increments to prevent the bright background recording grey.

The second set of photographs was taken using flash, with the unit hand-held at 45° and within 5 cm (2 in) of the slide. This powerful flash had to be so close because the microscope was magnifying (x30) only a minute portion of the slide whereas the flash was lighting not only the whole slide but the area around it too.

The final photographs were taken using traditional darkfield illumination, utilising the microscope's own light source but blocking the central rays and allowing only the peripheral rays through. These are too oblique to enter the objective lens direct and the only light reaching it is that scattered by the specimen, resulting in a brightly lit specimen on a black background. The blocking of the central rays was achieved by placing an opaque disc (a one pound coin – 22mm diameter – worked well) in the centre of the glass filter holder below the condenser.

This is an absorbing assignment with lots of scope for experimentation. Try using pairs of colour filters (red and green, yellow and blue) – they will produce very attractive (if somewhat unnatural) results.

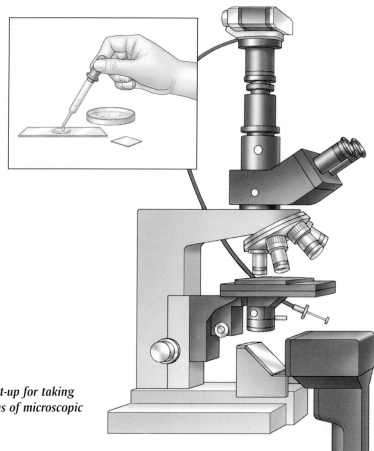

A typical set-up for taking photographs of microscopic specimens.

EQUIPMENT

MICROSCOPE

OLYMPUS OM2n BODY

METZ 45 FLASH UNIT

POND WATER

SLIDES, FILTERS

FUJI VELVIA 50 FILM

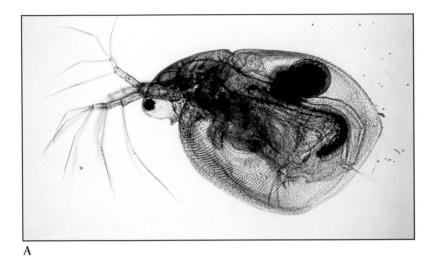

A

B

C

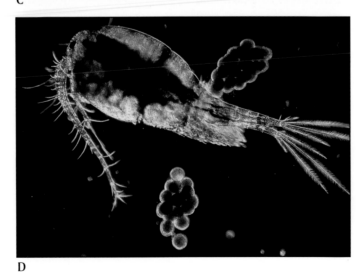

D

A. Above left: Daphnia lit using standard brightfield illumination, by bouncing the flash off a 45° half-silvered mirror. Because the flash light came up through the iris diaphragm and the sub-stage condenser, the former was adjusted to obtain the best compromise between depth of field and resolution, bearing in mind that the 'aperture' of the objective lens is controlled by the sub-stage iris diaphragm setting. Exposure: flash, +1 1/3 stops overexposure. Magnification x30. Fuji Velvia 50.

B. Above right: Daphnia lit using darkfield illumination in which the central rays are blocked by a darkfield stop, resulting in a black background. The scattering and reflection of the light by the water flea has highlighted the fine striations on its shell. Due to the long exposure the continuously beating filter-feeding appendages are recorded as little more than a blur – in contrast to the sharpness of the flash-lit photographs with their 1/1000 sec or less exposure. Exposure: 1/2 sec, –1 stop underexposure. Magnification x30. Fuji Velvia 50.

C. Centre: Daphnia lit by 45° flash side lighting, digestive tract and eggs clearly visible. Because the flash was directed onto the top of the water flea and did not come through the iris diaphragm, the objective lens could not be stopped down. As a result, the depth of field is very shallow indeed but where the image is in focus, the definition is excellent. Exposure: flash, –2/3 stop underexposure. Magnification x30. Fuji Velvia 50.

TIPS

❖ Slides and cover slips should be scrupulously clean as any grease marks are exaggerated when using incident, oblique and darkfield lighting.

❖ Experiment with different sized coins to produce the most effective darkfield effect, while leaving the sub-stage iris diaphragm wide open.

❖ Different colours can be introduced by using colour filters on the light source, resulting in a brightly coloured water flea against a black background.

D. Left: Cyclops, a common inhabitant of ponds, photographed live using darkfield illumination. Interesting features include the famous large single eye in the centre of the head, the two large egg sacs and the birefringent bristles on the tail which split the light into the colours of the spectrum. Exposure: 1/2 sec, –1 stop underexposure. Magnification x30. Fuji Velvia 50.

MICROSCOPIC LIFE

The sheer beauty of microscopic plants and animals will be revealed in this workshop, using materials available in any pond.

The most conspicuous plant material in many ponds is filamentous green algae (resembling cotton wool), consisting of long filaments of repeating cells, each with a nucleus and several green chloroplasts. Common examples include Spirogrya, which has a spiral chloroplast, Cladophora, a branching alga and Zygnema with its star-shaped chloroplasts. Also present are microscopic desmids and the exquisitely beautiful diatoms.

Pond water is teeming with a rich variety of microscopic animals, including the single-celled protozoans where all the bodily functions such as respiration, digestion, excretion etc. take place in one cell, plus the ciliates and the rotifers.

A small jar filled with pond water and filamentous algae will provide sufficient material for many hours of microscope work which will be as exciting as it is time-consuming.

I began by spreading a tiny piece of green, slimy alga on a glass slide, protected it with a cover slip and proceeded to examine it methodically using low magnification (x3 objective and x10 eyepiece). This provided a large field of view at low magnification but allowed the detection of any moving organisms.

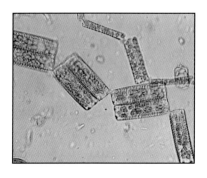

Diatoms with hard, flinty walls come in many shapes and sizes. The larger zigzag filament is Tabellaria, the smaller one is a similar species called Diatoma. Flash. Magnification x400.

Volvox colony surrounded by filamentous green algae. The colony consists of many hundreds of bi-flagellate cells whose movements cause the colony to rotate and roll. Magnification x40.

If the little creature is still too tiny and warrants closer examination, rotate the microscope nosepiece bringing the x10 objective lens into use, giving a total magnification of x100. Very occasionally the x40 objective lens can be used, but the x400 magnification, wonderful though it is, is at the expense of an extremely shallow depth of field. The latter can be increased by reducing the diameter of the iris diaphragm below the condenser lens but eventually the definition suffers as diffraction becomes a significant factor. Although the microscopic animals and plants were examined and focused using the microscope's inbuilt light

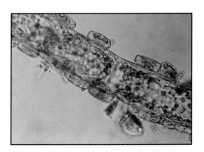
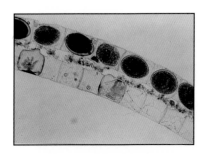

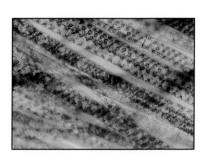

Filamentous alga with the green chloroplasts clearly visible. Adhering to the outer wall are several pill-box shaped diatoms with hard flinty walls. Flash. Magnification x400.

Reproduction in filamentous algae. Two filaments have come together and the contents of each cell have passed through a linking tube. Flash. Magnification x100.

Closterium is one of the best known desmids by virtue of its curved, moon-shaped cell. Flash. Magnification x400.

Strands of filamentous green algae, including Spirogyra – uninteresting to the naked eye but full of beauty and detail when magnified. Flash. Magnification x100.

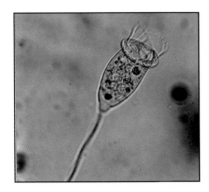

Vorticella, the 'bell animal', is common in still water attached to plants via a contractile stem. Flash. Magnification x100.

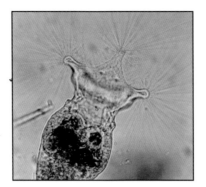

Collotheca, one of the 500 or so species of rotifer found in Britain. Most are free-living with a crown of short cilia. Flash. Magnification x100.

Hydra vulgaris is a tiny freshwater polyp, which has the ability to develop new bodies when broken up into small pieces. Flash. Magnification x4.

source (projected up through the 45° half-silvered mirror), the photographs were taken using flash (pointing horizontally and reflecting some of its light off the 45° half-silvered mirror up through the microscope and eventually into the camera). I used a TTL lead to link the flash unit to the camera but had already done some bracketing on the last few frames of the previous film to establish the best exposure (+ 1 1/3 stops) for the brightfield illumination system.

This is probably a new area of interest to most nature photographers, but it is well worth investing in a decent-quality microscope (not too expensive), which will allow you to enjoy the engrossing and exciting world of living micro-organisms.

TIPS

❖ Always use freshly cleaned slides and, if possible, new cover slips. Dust, dirt and grease will all be exaggerated and magnified.

❖ Look at the microscope from the side and, with the lowest power objective lens in place, rack down until it is within a few millimetres of the slide. Look down the eyepiece and rack up into focus. Never rack down as it usually results in a cracked slide.

❖ It is always worthwhile stopping down the sub-stage iris diaphragm to increase the depth of field but don't overdo it because the definition will begin to fall off as diffraction sets in.

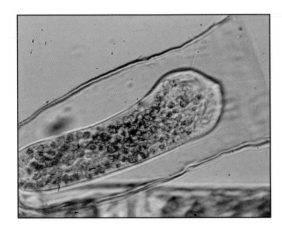

Dinobryon is a flagellate and in common with other members of the group represents the borderline between plants and animals. Flash, magnification x400

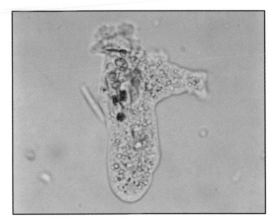

Amoeba proteus is arguably the best known of all protozoans and can usually be found on the surface of mud at the bottom of ponds. Visible inside it are some black and a few green, food particles. Flash. Magnification x400.

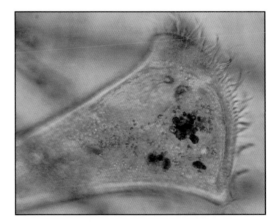

The 'trumpet animal', Stentor polymorphus, has a ring of cilia around the trumpet end which beat rapidly, sweeping food particles into the body. Flash. Magnification x400.

CHRISTMAS CACTUS

To photograph a Christmas Cactus Schlumbergera truncata flower highlighting not only its exquisite overall beauty, but enhancing if possible the almost fluorescent nature of the petals, is the aim of this assignment. There are only three recognised species of Schlumbergera but many hybrids, and those which flower around the Festive Season are normally referred to as Christmas cacti. By the time I got around to photographing the cactus, many of the flowers, particularly near the top, were already dying back, fortunately there were still one or two in full bloom lower down. Despite my best efforts, a suitable flower which formed a good, simple composition couldn't be found, I therefore had little choice but to detach a flower and a piece of forked stem and arrange them away from the parent plant. A mottled green board was positioned approximately 1.5 metres (59 in) behind the flower to form a suitable background.

To obtain a good-sized image of the flower, a 28mm extension tube was added to the 100mm macro lens. The lighting was a combination of weak daylight and overhead fluorescent lights and, although the flower looked reasonably attractive in the viewfinder, I decided to backlight the material using a small hand-held video light. A pale blue filter over the light eliminated the sickly yellow cast associated with artificial lighting on daylight-balanced film. An aperture of f 22 was used with auto-exposure bracketing up and down by 1 stop.

After making several exposures I looked at the flower again, discovering that the underside was also very attractive. The material was re-arranged and several more exposures were made.

This workshop assignment calls for good close-up technique with the ability to maximise on the zone of sharp focus in order to render pin-sharp the flower petals. An eye for composition is also important, but any experienced photographer should be able to produce similarly satisfying images without too much difficulty. You might try different lighting arrangements, including grazed lighting, in addition to the backlighting mentioned above.

The underside of the flower shows clearly the floral symmetry with the stamens and pollen-covered pistil clearly visible. The tilt of the flower makes a more interesting composition, while the flattened green segments, again backlit, form a frame around the top of the picture. Darkening tone towards the bottom of the flower and background forms a solid base to the picture. Exposure: 4 sec, f 22. 100mm macro lens. 28mm extension tube. Fuji Velvia.

EQUIPMENT

BRONICA ETRSi
MEDIUM FORMAT SLR
100MM MACRO LENS
E-28 AUTO-EXTENSION TUBE
SMALL VIDEO LIGHT
BACKGROUND BOARD, TRIPOD
FUJI VELVIA ISO 50 FILM

The long tubular flower was kept in sharp focus by setting it parallel to the film plane and stopping down to f 22, with the slightly upward tilt suggesting a flower at the peak of its development. Although not a strong saturated red, the flower is sufficiently red to 'advance' it and allow it to appear a little closer to the viewer. This separates it from the green background, which like blue, but to a much less degree, is a 'receding' colour. Exposure: 4 sec, f 22. 100mm macro lens. 28mm extension tube. Fuji Velvia.

TIPS

❖ Look for a fully-formed, perfect flower – if necessary remove one from the plant – the flowers all die eventually.

❖ A detached piece of stem can help the composition.

❖ A hand-held video light suitably filtered (piece of blue acetate sheet) will add general sparkle or can be used to backlight the flower.

❖ Choose a background colour which harmonises with the flower but is non-intrusive.

HONESTY IN AUTUMN

The aim of this workshop exercise is to produce interesting images of honesty where a sense of graphic design rather than colour and three-dimensional solidarity, is the main element in the composition.

The oval disc-shaped seedpods are green initially but as the seeds ripen, the pods lose their colour becoming quite translucent. When completely dry the outer membranes curl back and eventually drop off, exposing the seeds which fall to the ground as the plant is disturbed by the wind or passing animals. Photographed indoors from material collected locally in late September, the specimens selected had dried out and become translucent but still contained all six seeds.

The more powerful T32 flash unit was positioned 25cm (10 in) above and behind the honesty pod, with the lower-powered T20 flash used to lighten the background and to put a little detail onto the front surface of the specimen. It was positioned approximately 46cm (18 in) in front of the pod which was itself 50cm (20 in) from the background board.

Different backgrounds were used with exposures varying from normal to –1 stop, all at f 16. The Kodak Elite 50 transparency film was set at ISO 64.

This is a straightforward studio assignment which can be done at leisure, allowing plenty of time to arrange the plant material and experiment with the lighting. Having fulfilled the basic requirements of the assignment, I then tried to photograph seeds being dispersed before calling it a day.

EQUIPMENT

OLYMPUS OM2N

50MM MACRO LENS

T32 AND T20 FLASH UNITS

BACKGROUND BOARDS

TRIPOD AND CABLE RELEASE

KODAK ELITE ISO 50

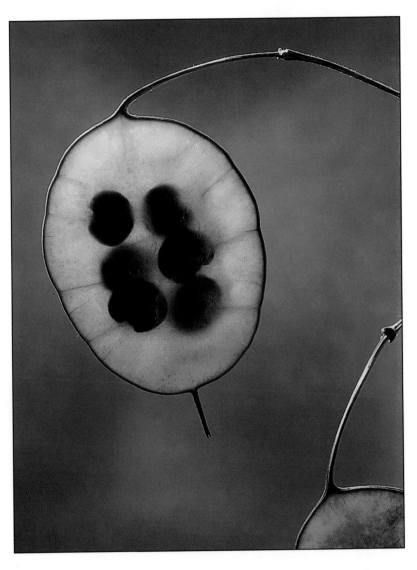

The composition is in the form of a reversed letter 'S' with the main area of interest, the seedpod, placed just above the centre of the frame, suggesting permanence (placed below the centre it would appear to be slipping out of the frame). I set up the specimen parallel to the film plane ensuring excellent definition across the seedpod and stalk. The high backlighting is shining strongly through the three-layered, paper-thin pod while rim lighting the top of the pod and its adjoining stalk. This helps to isolate the material from the background, which is in subdued harmonising browns and greens. Exposure: flash, f 16, –2/3 stop underexposure. 50mm macro lens. Kodak Elite 50.

In this shot I attempted to illustrate seed dispersal and show the general arrangement of the seedpods. The lighting set-up is similar to the first photograph, i.e. strong side/backlighting, with a lower-power fill-in frontal light. The dispersal effect was produced by selecting honesty in which the seeds were exposed and ready to drop and tapping the specimen with a pencil while almost simultaneously triggering the shutter and flash units using a cable release.

The arrangement, although quite natural, appears rather haphazard, and being positioned right in the centre of the frame looks a little boring. However several seeds, caught by the flash at differing angles, are clearly visible, which was the main purpose of the exercise. Exposure: flash, f 16, –2/3 stop underexposure. 50mm macro lens. Kodak Elite 50.

TIPS

❖ Always use complete, undamaged pods. Although damaged ones occur naturally, they look rather ugly in a photograph.

❖ Set the film plane (camera back) parallel to the pod to ensure good definition right across the frame.

❖ Artificial light can be used to illuminate the seedpods, but raise the colour temperature by holding a piece of blue acetate sheet in front of the light source.

RED CAMPION SEED DISPERSAL

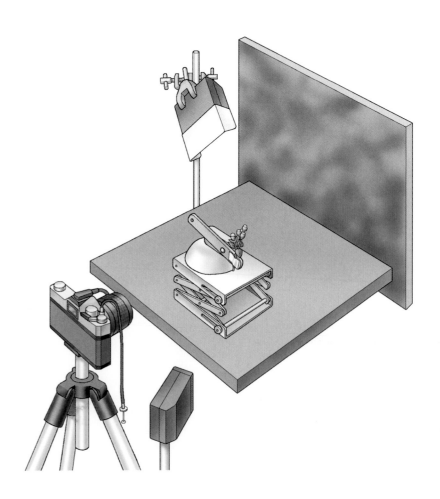

T he purpose of this workshop is to try to capture red campion seeds being thrown out of the seed box, with everything, except the escaping seeds, rendered bitingly sharp and nicely framed.

The selected specimen, consisting of several leaves and two capsules, was carefully checked to ensure that the seeds were ripe and loose, ready for dispersal. The material, supported in a laboratory clamp and stand, was tilted slightly not only to produce a satisfactory composition but to make it easier for the seeds to be released.

The seed boxes were lit using a powerful Olympus T32 flash unit 22cm (9 in) above and slightly behind, with the less powerful T20 flash unit 30cm (12 in) in front and to the right of the specimens, while a paint-sprayed background board was placed about 50cm (20 in) behind. My original method for taking the photograph was to tap the plant stem with a pencil, almost simultaneously pressing the cable release which tripped the shutter and fired the two flash units.

This method was neither reliable nor predictable. For my second attempt the campion was attached to one end of a small 15cm (6 in) see-saw and pre-focused on the capsule while the free end of the see-saw was held down. It was then returned to the resting position, and the capsules topped up with seeds. A sharp tap on the free end brought the campion capsules up into focus throwing out some seeds. Firing the flash was as described above.

The process was then repeated using different specimens arranged so that the camera was looking into the top of the capsule. When the free end of the see-saw was smartly pressed down, the seeds were thrown diagonally forwards. As we normally scan a picture from left to right, we meet the seeds heading towards us. Despite the very vigorous movement of the see-saw, the powerful flash units have resulted in an exposure sufficiently short to 'freeze' the capsules and keep them in sharp focus. Note the well defined striations on the seeds in the capsules. Exposure: flash, f16, -2/3 stop underexposure, 50mm macro lens, 25mm extension tube, Kodak Ektachrome 64.

EQUIPMENT

OLYMPUS OM2n CAMERA

50MM F3.5 MACRO LENS

25MM EXTENSION TUBE

TWO OLYMPUS FLASH UNITS

EKTACHROME 64 SLIDE FILM RATED AT ISO 80

The high backlighting not only highlights the capsules but puts a rim of light around the tops of the seeds, lifting them away from the background. The lower-powered fill-in flash has lit the otherwise dark frontal surfaces of the capsules. By moving the flash units further away, the longer exposure has given the seeds comet-like tails suggesting fast movement. But, as the equipment had leading curtain synch flash, the seeds appear to be whizzing back towards the capsules! Exposure: flash, f 16, –2/3 stop underexposure. 50mm macro lens. Kodak Ektachrome 64.

TIPS

❖ Check that the capsules are undamaged (they are often chewed by insect grubs) and ripe (i.e. full of loose seeds).

❖ Collect a number of spare specimens, tapping the capsules over a dish to collect the seeds, which can be used to top up the capsules after each exposure.

❖ Make sure the film plane is parallel to the see-saw, confirming that the capsules are in sharp focus by gently holding down the free end of the see-saw.

CREEPING THISTLE SEED DISPERSAL

T he aim of this assignment is to try to capture the delicate 'parachute' seeds of the thistle suspended in mid-air, well positioned in the frame and in sharp focus. Quite a tall order!

The deep purple flowers are visited regularly by bees searching for nectar, while unwittingly carrying pollen from flower to flower which fertilises the tiny ovule at the bottom of each floret. The developing seed is surrounded by a thin fruit coat attached to a very delicate hairy pappus. In damp weather the pappi remain tightly folded, but in warm sunny weather the dead flower-head dries and splits, the hairy pappi expand like parachutes and are carried away on the wind.

Some pieces of thistle were arranged to make a satisfactory composition and taped to a piece of cardboard. A strong backlight was supplied by a Metz 45 CL3 flash unit positioned some 13 in (33cm) above and behind the thistles with the flash carefully shielded to prevent any stray light falling on the camera lens. A piece of crumpled kitchen foil angled at around 45° and placed 8 in (20cm) in front of the thistles provided a little frontal fill-in lighting. As I wanted the very delicate parachute seeds to stand out against the background, black velvet was hung about 24 in (60 cm) behind the thistles.

I had photographed the thistles before, but experienced great difficulty co-ordinating the blowing of the flower head to release the parachutes with the tripping of the camera shutter and flash unit. Could I counterbalance their weight with an up-current of warm air, reasoning that if the two were about equal, the parachute seed would be suspended almost motionless?

The theory was that the holes in the tray would allow the warm air to come through in a smooth laminar flow which would help to keep the parachute seeds in one plane. The first ones shot upwards at great speed – too much hot air! Extinguishing the candle and waiting a few moments for the tray to cool down a little worked, and the parachutes hovered, allowing me to take a couple of shots. This was repeated several times, hoping that one frame would include the parachute seeds well positioned and in sharp focus.

This is another absorbing project calling for considerable skill in close-up work, lots of patience and the ability to anticipate exactly the right moment to release the shutter and flash unit.

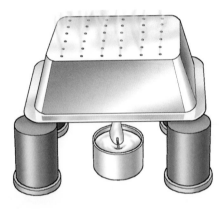

The set consisted of the thistle flowers arranged in line and backlit using a Metz 45 flash unit, with a reflector to provide some frontal fill-in lighting. A few small holes were punched in the bottom of a tinfoil tray (courtesy of the local Chinese take-away) which was inverted and supported at the corners on empty 35mm cassette tubes. Finally a small night-light candle was lit and placed under the tray.

EQUIPMENT

BRONICA ETRSi

6 x 4.5 CM MEDIUM FORMAT

100MM MACRO LENS

METZ 45, BLACK VELVET, TRIPOD

REFLECTOR, PLANT MATERIAL

FUJI PROVIA ISO 100 FILM.

The composition is satisfactory with the seeded flower head and the purple flowers below located at the strong points in the frame, leaving a relatively small area for the parachute seeds, which are fully open and perfectly positioned. The strong backlighting is quite dramatic with both the flower head and the two parachute seeds attractively lit and standing out from the background. The aluminium foil reflector has just put sufficient light onto the frontal surfaces to prevent the thistles becoming mere silhouettes. To be critical, due to slight overexposure of the seeded flower head, some detail has been lost and I wonder whether the black background is too severe and should have been replaced by something a little lighter, including some subdued colour. Exposure: flash, f 22, –1 stop underexposure. 100mm macro lens. Fuji Provia 100.

TIPS

❖ When collecting the thistles, look for complete flower heads with the parachute seeds fully formed and ready for dispersal.

❖ If the collected material is slightly damp, warming it up indoors will cause the 'dead' flower heads to expand and burst open quite quickly, as the parachutes unfold ready for dispersal.

❖ Taping the thistles to a piece of cardboard will not only stabilise the set-up, but everything will be in the same plane and therefore in sharp focus. A small lens aperture will increase the depth of field which is quite shallow when working in close-up.

LEAPING TREE FROG

T he aim of this workshop is to capture on film a tree frog leaping towards the camera (or the viewer) with as much as possible of its body (but certainly the eyes) in sharp focus. The frog must be well positioned in the frame with the overall composition adequate, at the very least.

The flight tunnel consists of a wooden-framed box 30cm (12 in) square at the front, rising to 45cm (18 in) high and 40cm (16 in) wide at the rear. The unit is approximately 60cm (24 in) long.

Pieces of white card were cut to size and pinned inside the wooden frame to enclose the bottom, sides and roof. A transparent acetate sheet was mounted in a cardboard frame to form the front. A selection of backgrounds were cut to size, spray-painted, and the appropriate one slipped into the rear of the tunnel.

The light beam was directed through a window in the side of the flight tunnel onto a mirror located outside a similar window on the opposite side. The beam was reflected back to a second mirror which in turn directed it onto the light-sensitive switch unit.

I now use an infrared beam switching device, manufactured by the French company Jama and marketed in Britain by Jamie Wood Products Ltd. The infrared receiver is linked through a lead and 2.5mm jack plug to the socket on the Olympus autowinder. Early flash units have now been replaced by Olympus T32s connected to the camera through TTL leads.

The time interval between breaking the beam and the exposure being made is a slow 1/25 sec in most SLR cameras and this must be taken into account by setting the beam some distance (around 5 cm for the tree frog) behind the pre-focused point. Unfortunately this distance cannot be calculated accurately as the frog does not leap at exactly the same speed each time.

The tiny frog, which had been kept for an hour or so among freshly cut green grass and was therefore a rich green colour, was lifted onto a small platform attached near the top of the side wall at the far end of the flight tunnel. Some live maggots bought from a local angling shop were placed in a shallow open dish near to the camera. I then sat back and waited for it all to happen!

After some minutes the wriggling maggots caught the attention of the frog which made a sudden leap in that direction, missing both the light beam and the maggots but landing safely on a branched

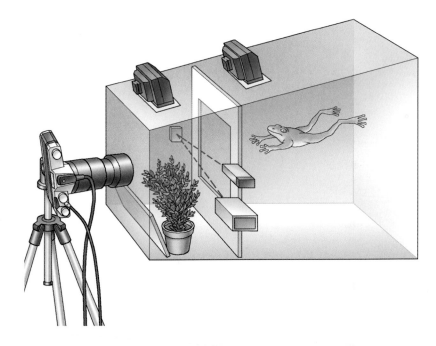

The home-made flight tunnel has been used over several years to take photographs of butterflies, moths, bees and damselflies in flight. The home-made light beam, receiver and triggering units have now been replaced by a more efficient infrared system which can also be used in the field. Success rate is only about 5 per cent.

twig strategically positioned near to the camera. I returned the frog to its platform and waited.

Over the next two hours or so, the frog made several jumps, often breaking the light beam and triggering the camera and flash units. This type of work requires lots of patience coupled with the certainty that around 95 per cent of the frog images would be slightly out of focus or badly positioned in the frame, yet one sharp, well-framed image would more than justify all the time and effort put into the project.

If you are prepared to construct a simple flight tunnel and either build the light beam switching equipment, or buy the excellent Jama unit, you are well placed to make a useful attempt. Tree frogs are not always available but the common frog will serve equally well and with care and a bit of luck (yes, luck does play a part) an exciting leaping frog picture could be added to your library of images.

EQUIPMENT

MAMIYA 645 MEDIUM FORMAT
SLR CAMERA

75MM TOMINON ENLARGING LENS

BELLOWS UNIT, FLIGHT TUNNEL

INTERRUPTED
LIGHT BEAM EQUIPMENT

THREE T32 FLASH UNITS, TRIPOD

KODAK EKTACHROME 64 FILM

This shot is very dynamic with the little frog's limbs stretched to the absolute limit as it leaps towards the camera lens. Fortunately the zone of sharp focus extends right across the left forelimb with the digits and sucker pads clearly defined. The all-important eye is clearly visible but the hindlimbs are running out of focus.

The plant stems help to frame the picture, the background colours harmonise well with the frog's skin and are sufficiently dark in tone to allow the frog to stand out. Exposure: multiple flash, f 11/ f 16. 75mm enlarging lens. Kodak Ektachrome 64.

TIPS

❖ Get on friendly terms with the local pet shop owner and he might let you borrow a frog for a few days.

❖ This assignment calls for lots of time and patience (I think I've said that before – several times!)

❖ Tree frogs need a reason to get off their hind legs and leap. Food is the best inducement.

FLIGHT OF THE BUMBLEBEE

The goal of this workshop project will be (hopefully) a photograph of a bumblebee in flight using an exposure sufficiently short to 'freeze' the wings, rendering them pin-sharp, while at the same time having enough depth of field to keep the bee's body and legs in sharp focus.

The bumblebee has a wing-beat of around 130 cycles per second with a straight-line speed of over 7 m.p.h. (10 k.p.h.) which can continue for about 15 minutes, after which it must stop to refuel by taking in energy-rich nectar. The photographs of the bumblebees were taken towards the end of August in the same flight tunnel used to photograph the leaping tree frog (page 152).

The flight tunnel was modified by reducing the rectangular aperture through which the insect flies from the original 20 x 15 cm to 15 x 10 cm, allowing me to set the camera closer and thereby produce a larger image on the transparency. To guide the bumblebee towards the aperture, a horizontal funnel-like lining was made from pieces of transparent acrylic sheeting (as used in DIY secondary double glazing) sellotaped in place.

A number of trial exposures using a wooden model indicated that the underside of the insect would be underlit; this was corrected by positioning a piece of kitchen-foil-covered cardboard at an angle of 45° in front of the aperture to reflect some light upwards. Spray-painted background boards had been used previously but on this occasion I also experimented with a photographic enlargement of an outside scene showing blue sky, clouds and out-of-focus purple heather in the lower part of the picture. Finally, some bell heather flowers were arranged just in front of the aperture and the tripod-mounted camera focused on them.

The infrared beam was set up approximately 2.5 cm behind the flowers and after crossing the aperture it was reflected off a mirror, back across the aperture to the receiver unit. The latter was linked by a lead to the 2.5mm input socket of the Olympus autowinder. The bumblebee was kept happy during its enforced change of environment by placing a small dish of sugar solution in the bottom of the tunnel but well out of frame. The bumblebee responded positively to the low-wattage electric light held at the camera end of the tunnel, flying through the aperture, and sometimes breaking the IR beam and triggering the shutter and the three flash units.

A major problem soon emerged: how to retrieve the bee once it had flown through the aperture into the sealed front section of the

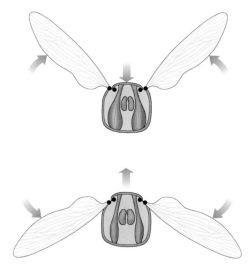

Control of wing movements in insect flight. Contraction of the vertical flight muscles pulls down the roof (tergum) of the thorax which, pressing on the very short end of a lever system, forces the wing upwards. When the longitudinal flight muscles contract, the tergum bulges upward forcing the wing down. Rotation of the wings is controlled by other smaller muscles.

tunnel. After much thought and experimentation, I came up with a small device consisting of an empty matchbox attached by a blob of flexible adhesive (silicone sealer) to the end of a length of wire. After drilling a small hole near the top and another towards the bottom of the front panel, a matchbox/wire device was slid through each hole and the panel returned to the front of the tunnel. Wherever the bee alighted there was a 'matchbox catcher' nearby to cover the bee and carefully move it to the aperture, when it would fly into the main body of the tunnel, ready to face the camera again.

The 80mm macro lens was set at f 16, using aperture priority with −2/3 stop underexposure. Of the 72 frames I exposed over several days, about ten were in sharp focus but only two had the bumblebee reasonably well placed in the frame.

EQUIPMENT

OLYMPUS OM2n

80 MM MACRO LENS

TELESCOPIC AUTO-TUBE 65–116

TRIPOD, FLIGHT TUNNEL

IR BEAM SWITCH

KODAK ELITE ISO 100.

The wings are sharply defined, despite beating at more than 100 times per second, due to the extremely short flash duration (estimated at around 1/15,000 sec) produced by the powerful flash units placed so close to the subject. The bumblebee is flying across the frame and being parallel to the camera film plane, its entire body, from the short antennae to the hairs on the end of the abdomen, is in sharp focus. Clearly visible is the eye, complete with catchlight, while the third nearside leg shows the pollen comb and the pollen basket immediately above it. Exposure: multiple flash, f 16, −2/3 stop underexposure. 80mm macro lens. Kodak Elite 100.

TIPS

❖ Experiment with the set-up using the last few frames on a roll of film, making any adjustments to exposure or distances before committing yourself to a whole film and hours of work.

❖ Careful, delicate handling of the bees and equipment, plus infinite patience are the hallmarks of this assignment.

❖ Study the bee's flight patterns before finally deciding on the distance between the beam and the point of focus – a slow flyer obviously requires a shorter distance.

The bee is flying towards the camera with its abdomen hanging down slightly, requiring critical focusing and the largest possible depth of field to keep it all in sharp focus. Luck was on my side as the point of focus and the depth of field are just right, resulting in a pin-sharp image from head to tail. The bee is well positioned, with the surrounding heather attractively framing the image, while the sky background looks pleasantly natural. To be critical, I would prefer the bee higher in the frame where it would look more dynamic and the heather flowers are unfortunately past their best. Exposure: multiple flash, f 16, −2/3 stop underexposure. 80mm macro lens. Kodak Elite 100.

BUTTERFLY WING

A butterfly wing can look very attractive even to the naked eye but when highly magnified it takes on a beauty which is truly amazing. To capture these exquisite images is the purpose of this assignment.

In flying insects the wings probably evolved as flaps, allowing the insect to leap away from danger and glide some distance. Over millions of years they slowly evolved into very efficient flying structures with the lightweight membranes strengthened by supporting veins.

In most butterflies and moths the wing membranes are neatly covered with minute overlapping scales (hence the Latin name Lepidoptera – 'scale wings'), not dissimilar to the slates on a house roof. Each is attached by a short peg which fits into a tiny socket on the wing surface. The pigments in these scales produce the beautiful wing colours and patterns, although some 'metallic' or 'iridescent' colours are the result of light being refracted by the minute ridges on the surface of the scales.

The peacock butterfly was found dead, trapped in a spider's web in a corner of a window in the garage. A forewing was removed and carefully glued onto a piece of black cardboard which was then positioned vertically, using a pair of standard bench stands. Two T32 flash units were set up at about 45° in front of and 45° above the wing to highlight the texture of the wing surface. The 80mm macro lens, stopped down to f 22 and mounted on a bellows unit, was moved in to approximately 6 cm from the wing and several shots were taken. I then switched to the 20mm macro lens and moved in even closer (3cm) after repositioning the flash units at a more grazing 30° angle to the wing. The smallest aperture available was f 16; at smaller apertures the definition would fall off as diffraction set in. A powerful reading lamp was held close to the wing to provide sufficient light to focus the lens.

The camera, bellows and lens were operated as one unit rather than racking the bellows back and forth, although the 80mm lens did have a helicoid fine focus system. The 20mm lens did not, and just to make life more difficult, it had to be stopped down manually.

This is a very advanced assignment where image sharpness is all important, but with a depth of field of less than 1mm, critical focusing becomes the key requirement.

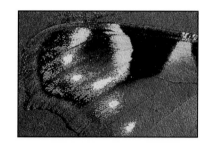

The photograph of the complete wing has been included for reference purposes to show the overall colour pattern, although it is sufficiently magnified (x2) to make the scales just visible, helped by the semi-grazed lighting. Exposure: flash, f 22. 80mm macro lens. Bellows unit. Fuji Velvia 50.

This image shows an area near the wingtip magnified approximately x5, and working at this magnification, my efforts had been well worthwhile in just producing an image so sharply defined. The slight backlash in the rack-and-pinion focusing system was sufficient, despite my best efforts, to throw several images slightly out of focus. The image is very acceptable because of the attractive range of colours, with the lighter, brighter tones towards the top of the frame. Exposure: flash, f 16. 20mm macro lens. Bellows unit. Fuji Velvia 50.

EQUIPMENT

OLYMPUS OM2n

80MM F4 ZUIKO MACRO LENS

20MM F3.5 ZUIKO MACRO LENS

AUTO-BELLOWS UNIT, TRIPOD

TWO OLYMPUS T32 FLASH UNITS

VELVIA ISO 50 FILM.

TIPS

 The biggest problem is aligning the wing absolutely parallel to the film plane (camera back). This is easier if you have a macro stand or optical bench – I don't have either.

 At high magnifications with a stopped-down lens, the view-finder brightness (or lack of it) makes focusing very difficult. Use a powerful light to illuminate the specimen while focusing.

 Accurate focusing is critical. Any backlash in the system can throw the image right out of focus – make plenty of exposures and hope your luck is in!

The final image (magnification x8) was again the only one of half a dozen exposures to be in sharp focus. The individual scales are neatly arranged in rows and clearly defined, while at the bottom left some of the tiny attachment pegs and sockets left behind after scales have become detached are clearly visible. The diagonal line-up of the scales makes a more interesting image than a purely horizontal treatment. Again, the dark area at the bottom of the frame provides a satisfactory base to a picture which I think represents sheer beauty at micro level. The peacock butterfly had obviously died towards the end of a long season as shown by the damaged wing membranes and the loss of many of the scales. Exposure: flash, f16. 20mm macro lens. Bellows unit. Fuji Velvia 50.

FIELD MOUSE

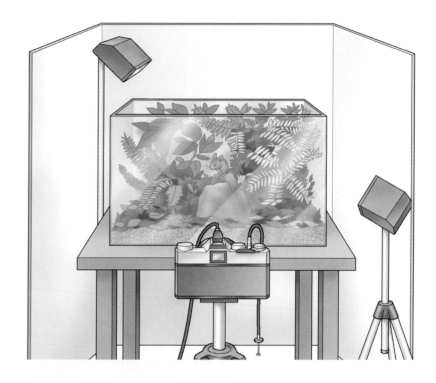

The aim of this assignment is to produce appealing, active shots of a field mouse against a natural-looking background.

The mouse was caught in a Longworth small mammal trap. On entering the short 13cm (5 in) tunnel in search of food, the mouse activated a trip bar which closed the flap door behind it. Moving into the second part of the trap – the nest box – it fed on the food placed there and then curled up in the bedding material where it remained until the trap was examined the following morning. After the photography had been completed the mouse was returned, fit and well, to the spot where I caught it.

I normally use a glass aquarium measuring 45 x 30 x 30 cm (18 x 12 x 12 in) complete with a glass top. The floor was covered with dead leaves, pieces of bark and moss, while an old stump was set up in the centre. The background consisted of pieces of fern, bracken and blackberry twigs attached to a dark green background board, in an attempt to replicate the natural environment of the mouse.

The lighting was arranged as it might have been in the wild, with the main flash unit (the sun) near one end but above and towards the front of the aquarium. A second flash unit was positioned at the other end of the aquarium just above ground level, to act as a fill-in light. The camera, linked to the two flash units by TTL leads, was hand-held so that I could follow the mouse around the aquarium, although this did call for quick focusing and framing.

Finally a piece of black cardboard approximately 30 cm (12 in) square, with a circular hole cut in the centre, was carefully pressed onto the lens barrel. This prevented reflections of the camera and myself appearing in the front glass of the aquarium. If the camera lens is almost touching the aquarium glass and parallel to it, then the glass will function as a plane glass filter and the camera will in effect have 'penetrated' the aquarium. However the front glass must be of a high quality and free from blemishes and surface dirt and grease.

This workshop assignment is quite tricky, requiring careful handling of the mouse but any reasonably competent photographer who has either a macro lens, extension tubes or supplementary lenses for close-up work and is prepared to invest in a live mammal trap, should find it a worthwhile challenge. The same set-up can be used to photograph hamsters, gerbils or voles.

The Longworth small mammal trap contains food, water and bedding for the overnight stay

EQUIPMENT

OLYMPUS OM2n

50MM MACRO LENS

TWO T32 FLASH UNITS

AQUARIUM AND VARIOUS PIECES OF PLANT MATERIAL

KODAK ELITE ISO 100 FILM

The composition is quite symmetrical with the mouse perched on top of the conical tree-stump. The position of the mouse could be criticised as being too central but I thought this was acceptable so that the whole tail could be included. Also because of the closeness of the mouse to the background, the ferns and bracken could be considered to be too sharply defined and somewhat distracting. Exposure: two flash units, f 16. 50mm macro lens. Kodak Elite 100.

TIPS

❖ A Longworth Trap (available from Philip Harris Ltd, see appendix) is essential to catch small rodents, alive and unhurt.

❖ The accepted way of handling a mouse is by holding its tail; it looks inelegant but it works.

❖ Mice are very fast movers and jumpers but a supply of food (mixed seeds) will hold their attention, causing them to rest while eating.

❖ Always use a black card pressed onto the lens barrel to eliminate reflections in the front glass of the aquarium, which should be clean and free from in-built blemishes.

An attractive picture with the mouse in the classic sitting position amply supported on its elongated feet, while it assiduously cleans its front paws. Due to the side-on position of the mouse and the well stopped down lens, the eye, whiskers and fur are all sharply defined. A better composition would have been achieved with the mouse moved a little to the right giving more space for it to look into. Unfortunately the dark red leaf stalk behind the mouse's nose is a slight distraction.
Exposure: two flash units, f 16. 50mm macro lens. Kodak Elite 100.

CHAPTER ELEVEN

Patterns & Abstracts

Wildlife photography is by its very nature principally about creating images of animals and plants which are easily recognised by their shape, size, colour and texture. However, there is an area of nature photography which explores patterns and abstract images.

Although patterns do not always involve repetition (a sea urchin, for example, viewed from above exhibits radial symmetry, a pattern which is quite obvious but non-repeating), it is generally accepted that most patterns are created by the apparent or implied repetition of shapes, lines, colours and textures. Some patterns are transient, such as the ripples on a lake or the light and shade on a landscape as clouds pass over the sun, but their impact can be just as strong and their emotional content just as high as the more stable patterns of nature.

At one extreme the pattern may be so subtle that its existence is sensed only vaguely, whereas at the other, it may be manifestly obvious, hitting the viewer squarely between the eyes.

Patterns in the natural world are sometimes limited to a relatively small portion of the animal or plant and with the interest in the complete organism missing, the colours, lines and patterns must carry the whole weight of the photograph and be sufficiently strong to capture the attention of the viewer. The image should say something positive, which may be triggered by the juxtaposition of the colours or shapes or by something less tangible such as a subconscious thought or feeling based on some past event.

As we move in even closer to the plant, animal or bird, the images become less like the original, finally going completely abstract with no clues from the original organisms to help us. The intellectual and emotional response to the image will then rely solely on line and colour (or occasionally texture) as it becomes completely two-dimensional and graphic, with depth playing little or no part.

As many of the sections in this chapter are very short, consisting of an image and its caption, the cameras and lenses used have been brought together and listed opposite, to avoid the unnecessary repetition of an equipment 'box' appearing on every page.

SUGGESTIONS

❖ Although patterns and abstract images are very widespread in nature, you need a 'seeing eye' to find them. When examining plant or animal material which may have caught your attention, hold a 35 mm transparency mount between your eye and the subject, moving it slowly back and forth to alter the framing and composition until you produce a satisfactory image.

❖ While many patterns and abstract images do occur at macro-level, others exist at the other end of the size spectrum.

❖ Try scanning an area of coniferous woodland or a heather-covered moor using a 400 or 500 mm telephoto lens when the magnification and the very narrow angle of view will isolate very small sections of the landscape which could produce some interesting patterns or abstract images.

❖ A repeating pattern such as a carpet of bluebells might yield an unusual image by trying different focal length lenses from both the horizontal and overhead positions.

❖ Looking for abstract shapes and patterns in the natural world can be a fascinating pursuit; this is an area of nature photography where the images are limited only by your imagination and your ability to see beyond the obvious.

Interesting pattern of diagonal fissures in the bark of a sweetchestnut tree, with pleasantly harmonising greens and browns. Exposure: 1/60sec, f11, 50mm macro lens, Kodak Elite 100.

EQUIPMENT

OLYMPUS OM2n

28, 50, 300 MM LENSES

20, 50, 80 AND 90 MM MACRO LENSES

BRONICA ETRSi WITH 100 MM MACRO LENS

PENTAX 645 WITH STANDARD 80 MM LENS

T32 FLASH. MICROSCOPE X 40 MAGNIFICATION

CROSSED POLARISERS.

Seashore patterns – with little depth or colour in the image, the interest must be generated by the shapes and textures of the triangular-sectioned Pomatoceros worm cases and the dead branching red alga, Corallina. Exposure: 1/30 sec, f 11. 90mm macro lens. Kodak Elite 50.

STONE WALLS

A major feature of the agricultural revolution in the sixteenth to eighteenth centuries was the thousands of private Enclosure Acts passed by Parliament, allowing the land to be divided up and enclosed by hedges, fences, walls or ditches to create fields. As a result, most of the countryside ceased to be 'common' land as it had been under the old feudal system of management and became owned by aristocratic families, merchants, lawyers, bankers and other wealthy groups.

In the Yorkshire Dales, for example, the grazing land was divided up into fields by drystone walls, which were built without any mortar or binding agent between the stones and courses. This task required great skill, but many of the limestone walls are still standing today as a testament to a now almost lost craft.

The drystone walls in the higher regions exposed to the elements are often devoid of any plant life, but the wall I photographed was located in a very sheltered area and had over many years become colonised by encrusting lichens and several species of moss. This photograph was taken mid-morning in bright sunlight using a 50mm macro lens on a tripod-mounted camera.

A typical drystone wall on limestone sediment rock high above Malham in the Yorkshire Dales. Exposure: 1/30 sec, f 11. 50mm lens. Fuji Velvia.

A repeating pattern of stones which might, at first sight, appear to be randomly arranged but on closer examination can be seen to be built in courses. I am drawn to the overall feeling of uniformity, with the individual stones covered in white and blue/green encrusting lichens, yet linked together by an interesting pattern of bright green mosses topped with dead pine needles. But what really brings the image to life is the grazed sunlight 'kissing' almost every stone and highlighting the texture of their surfaces. Exposure: 1/60 sec, f 11. 50mm macro lens. Kodak Elite 100.

LIMESTONE PAVEMENT

The Great Scar Limestone in the Yorkshire Dales is a 200 metre (650 ft) thick bed of sedimentary rock laid down over 300 million years ago in the warm shallow seas of the Carboniferous period. The marine sediment was compressed and crystallised to form hard limestone, overlaid by grits, sandstones and shales. During the various Ice Ages which began in the Pleistocene period some one million years ago, the surface layers of rock were ground off by the slow-moving glaciers, exposing large areas of limestone.

Rainwater containing carbon dioxide gradually dissolved parts of the limestone forming a landscape of crags, dry valleys, cave systems, potholes and underground streams, known as 'karst' (after a region in Yugoslavia).

The limestone pavement was formed when rainwater slowly opened up vertical crannies and crevices (grikes) in the rock and slightly rounded off and corrugated the surrounding blocks (clints) to produce relatively flat pavement reminiscent of the surface of an old Roman road. The well-shaded grikes house one or two special varieties of ferns and mosses, while the clints have encrusting lichens and mosses which thrive in the pollution-free atmosphere.

For this assignment I used an Olympus OM2n camera and a range of lenses, taking photographs from a variety of angles, including overhead shots from the top of a pair of folding steps.

An area of limestone pavement, part of the 'karst' landscape above the village of Malham in the Yorkshire Dales. Exposure: 1/8 sec, ƒ 16. 28mm lens. Fuji Velvia.

The limestone pavement contains very little colour but lots of interesting textures and shapes in the clints to hold the viewer's interest. The dark underlit grikes carry the eye through the scene, adding a sense of depth, while the clints, albeit of differing sizes and shapes, form a pattern of repeating units, with an overall feeling of solidarity and timelessness. Exposure: 1/2 sec, ƒ 22. 90mm macro lens. Fuji Velvia.

ORCHID

Orchids belong to the family Orchidaceae which contains some 18,000 species, distributed throughout the warmer parts of the world, particularly the damp equatorial regions. Many tropical orchids are epiphytes growing on trees, while the temperate members tend to grow on the ground. Over the years many hundreds of man-made hybrids have also been developed.

The flowers are occasionally solitary but are usually borne in spikes, racemes or panicles, on erect or drooping stems. Each flower has three petal-like sepals, alternating with three petals, the lowest of which can be spurred, pouched or crested, often with a fringed tongue-like extension. In the centre of the flower is an erect structure, the column, which bears the reproductive organs (stamen and ovary).

Some photographs were taken of the complete flower head, then I gradually moved in closer until finally only the central portion was filling the frame. For some shots natural daylight was used while for others, flash softened by a white handkerchief provided the illumination, with exposures ranging from 10 seconds at f 32 in daylight to less than 1/1000 second with flash.

Being so close to the orchid, the outline of the flower has been lost as we move towards a more abstract image where line and colour become increasingly important. I particularly like the bilateral symmetry of the image where the left side is a mirror image of the right and even the two-lobed stamen and fringed tongue-like extension are split perfectly symmetrically by an imaginary line running vertically down the centre of the frame. The lines of the petal margins lead the eye towards the centre of the image where the reproductive structures are located, with the deep cerise central petal adding some welcome weight to the lower part of the image. Exposure: flash, f 22. 80mm macro lens. Kodak 50. Singapore.

PINE LOG

The image of a small section of a pine log was taken in early spring with weak sunlight providing good overall illumination, at an angle just sufficient to highlight some of the surface texture. I am particularly attracted to the almost infinite variety of fascinating shapes displayed in warm, harmonising browns and oranges, which are built up in layers overlying the grey areas and giving the image a little depth. It brings to mind a small section of an oil painting where the palette knife has been freely used.

Below is the irregular, colourful, non-repeating pattern in the crumbling remains of a long-dead sweet chestnut tree.

Exposure: 1/60 sec, f 11. 50mm macro lens. Kodak Elite 100.

AUTUMN LEAVES

As the growing season draws to a close, the leaves, which have been manufacturing food for the tree throughout the spring and summer, have now become an embarrassment. They continue to give off water which the tree can ill afford to lose because the roots are now having difficulty obtaining water from the cold soil. The various pigments (including green chlorophyll) in the leaves have been broken down, with the useful substances taken back into the tree, while the residue (autumn tints) is left in the leaves. Finally a layer of corky tissue grows across the base of each leaf stalk and, with the help of the wind, the leaves are shed.

The second example shows flowering cherry, Prunus sargentii, leaves below the parent tree and was photographed with the camera looking directly down onto the leaves with the camera back parallel to the ground to ensure good definition across the frame.

The final shot, of sweet chestnut leaves, was taken early one morning in November as the overnight frost was beginning to melt in the bright sunshine. It too was taken from above to ensure adequate sharpness across the transparency.

Above: A simple shot of an irregular pattern consisting of similar-sized repeating units (leaves), so evenly spread as to produce an almost homogeneous carpet effect. The warm colours ranging from russet to amber and yellow are particularly attractive set against the harmonising green background. Exposure: 1/60 sec, f 11. 50mm lens. Kodak Elite 100.

Left: Multi-coloured carpet of Maple leaves photographed from above. Exposure: 1/60 sec, f 11. 50mm lens. Kodak Elite 100.

A random pattern made up of sweet chestnut, Castanea sativa, leaves lying on slightly undulating ground. I was particularly attracted to the warm browns in the leaves (suggesting mellow autumn days) and the melting ice crystals around the serrated leaf margins, midribs and leaf veins. The image is enhanced by the dappled light as the low early morning sun grazes the central leaves with the darker edges forming a frame to the picture. The spiky sweet chestnut fruit are well placed, adding a little more interest to the image without dominating it. Exposure: 1/2 sec, f 22. Bronica 100mm macro lens. Fuji Velvia.

ABSTRACT WOODLAND

On a still, windless day reflections in water are near perfect: very accurate, full of detail and differing from the original by being about one stop darker. As the surface becomes disturbed by the wind, the reflected image begins to break up until eventually in a strong breeze it may disappear completely.

In this assignment I made the reflected image fill the frame and become fairly abstract in an effort to produce a painted picture effect rather than a photograph. Exposures ranged from 2 seconds to 1/15 second, hoping that one would yield the image I was looking for. In the shot selected I have inverted the transparency to produce the desired effect.

The general atmosphere engendered is one of a tranquil woodland scene as might be painted by an artist who did not intend to make his work so naturalistic as to show every branch and twig in fine detail. He has nevertheless included much detail in the scene but in a slightly more abstract way. The browns, yellows and creams harmonise well and, as the photograph was taken in January, the trees (except for the occasional conifer) were bare, while the masses of dead bracken behind the trees still retained their rich autumn colours. The slight disturbance of the water, coupled with the particular exposure chosen, has resulted in a surface texture which is almost tactile. Exposure: 1/6 sec, f 11. 80mm lens. Pentax 645n camera, Fuji Velvia

LEAF SKELETON

If the autumn leaves are left on the ground, most slowly break up, some shrivel up but remain more or less intact, while a few, with more resistant stems and veins, partially disintegrate leaving behind an assortment of leaf skeletons.

A tree which displays interesting formations in its leaf skeletons is the Lombardy poplar, Populus nigra cv. Italica, a narrow columnar variant of the black poplar.

Several leaf skeletons were collected from the far end of our garden and examined to find an attractive skeletal pattern; not a boringly complete one but one with just enough small holes and fissures in it to make it interesting.

The leaf skeleton was pressed in a book for several days to flatten it, after which it was set up vertically with the camera back parallel to it to ensure image sharpness right across the frame. Strong backlighting was provided by a shielded unfiltered video light positioned above and behind the leaf, with a piece of dark brown card as a background.

One of the most attractive features of this image is the overall rich brown, almost luminous network of veins set against the harmonising dark brown background. The backlighting has highlighted the leaf veins leading the eye along them, exploring the myriad of interesting shapes and patterns en route, before finally arriving at one of the many dark holes. The distribution of these holes is satisfying, with a larger total area in the lower section of the frame, giving it some weight and stability. Exposure: 1/30 sec, f 16. 50mm macro lens. Kodak Ektachrome 64.

Moonscape

Moulds are micro-fungi belonging to the same group of plants as mushrooms, toadstools and puff-balls, sharing with them the inability to make their own food, as they do not possess the necessary green chlorophyll. Fungi obtain their food ready-made by growing on living organisms as parasites or on dead decaying animals and plants as saprophytes.

Another interesting feature common to all fungi is that they reproduce not by making seeds, but by producing millions of microscopic spores which are present in the air at all times but are much too small to be seen with the naked eye.

I grew the moulds for this abstract image by keeping a few slices of damp bread in a warm environment. Within a few days spores in the air had collected on the bread and begun to grow. The bread was then covered to prevent any minute mould threads and spores being dispersed around the kitchen and after about a week the mould was ready to be photographed. The mouldy bread was set up in various positions and, using bright sunlight as the only source of illumination, several photographs were taken with the 50mm macro lens on a tripod-mounted camera.

The mouldy bread ready to be photographed.

This is very much an abstract image and how you respond to it will depend on whether, either cerebrally or emotionally, you can connect with it. I see it as an other-worldly, slightly menacing image from an alien planet with the black recesses in the vertical 'cliff' face harbouring who knows what! Even the greens, browns and orange colours do not fit in with what we expect to see here on earth, while the bushes with their clusters of tiny balls suggest extra-terrestrial vegetation. Exposure: 1/8 sec, f 16. 50mm macro lens. Kodak Ektachrome 50.

BUTTERFLY
WING SCALES

The photograph was taken using the same set-up described in the earlier chapter 'Studio Workshop'. This is an abstract pattern as the shape of the butterfly wing has been completely lost leaving the image to stand or fall on its composition and the repeating pattern of the wing scales. The V-shaped configuration draws the eye from the top corners down through the frame with the block of black scales and the lighter scales above, balanced by a smaller group of black scales towards the top right of the frame. I find the perfect bilateral symmetry of each tooth-topped scale, the strong warm colours, and their precise linear alignment quite stunning.

Exposure: flash, f 16. 20mm macro lens. Fuji Velvia.

Exposure: 1/8 sec, f 16. 50mm macro lens. Kodak Ektachrome 100.

FERN FROND

The photograph of a group of lobes, which is part of the frond of the common bracken, Pteridium aquilinum, was taken indoors in natural sunlight supplemented by a powerful backlight. I am drawn to the elegant arc of the channelled stem and the symmetrical repeating pattern of the side lobes, but what really makes the image 'pop out' are the almost luminous yellows and browns enhanced by the bright rim lighting around the margins of the lobes. Much of the rich colouring is due to the low colour temperature of the unfiltered hand-held video light, which on this occasion works well, adding warmth to the basic colour of the autumn fern frond.

GREY GHOSTS

This image is abstract in extremis, with nothing sharply defined and no strong colours to stimulate the imagination. A longer look at it might suggest a group of animals or birds sheltering from the wind and rain. It is in fact part of a colony of grey seals on one of the rocky islands of the Outer Farnes, off the Northumberland coast. They are lying at the water's edge, surrounded by a filamentous green alga commonly known as sea-grass, but are quite unmoved by the constant pounding of the waves. The photograph was taken in poor light, from a small boat bobbing up and down on a heavy swell. I was using a 75–300mm zoom lens set at the 300mm mark with an exposure setting of 1/60 second on the hand-held camera. The abstract image is the result of too long an exposure for a 300mm hand-held lens, plus camera movement caused by the constant pitching of the boat.

I am attracted to the overall almost monotone greyness of the image, ranging from black through various shades of grey to almost white, and intrigued that the grey bodies have sharp ends, all pointing in the same direction even though the seals were quite haphazardly distributed on the shore. But the overall feeling is one of bleakness as I imagine tormented souls or creatures battling against the elements and possibly against life itself. Exposure: 1/60 sec, f 5.6. 300mm lens. Fuji Sensia 100.

SPECTRAL PHENOMENON

A polarising filter is normally used to reduce surface reflections in glass, water and polished wood and to darken blue sky or improve the colour saturation of grass. For this assignment two polarising filters were used: one (polariser) was placed over the light source under the microscope stage and the other (analyser) was fixed on top of the eyepiece. Certain crystals are birefringent and can rotate the plane of polarisation of light passing through them, some rotating it by different amounts for different colours. When one of these substances is positioned between two crossed polarisers (i.e. the top one rotated until the field goes almost black), it appears multicoloured against a black background.

An organic chemical called santanin (which was widely used in Africa to treat tapeworm infections) was smeared onto a slide, gently heated to melt it and then allowed to cool, when crystals began to form. Other substances which respond to cross-polarisation include citric acid (lemon juice), ascorbic acid (vitamin C), epsomite (epsom salts) and cellophane.

Several exposures were made from different sections of the slide using the photomicrographic equipment described in Chapter 4.

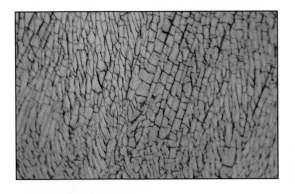

Crystals of santanin photographed without polarisation.

Crystals under cross-polarised light. In this abstract image I am attracted to the well-saturated spectral colours with the weird pointed tops suggesting distorted stained-glass windows in some ghostly church. Even the supporting 'lead' framework is misshapen adding to the bizarre nature of the image. Exposure: flash. Crossed polarisers. x40 magnification. Kodak Ektachrome 64.

APPENDIX

EQUIPMENT AND CAMERAS

M. Billingham & Co. Ltd., Little Cottage St., Brierley Hill, West Midlands, DY5 1RG. Tel: 01384 482828 *Camera bag manufacturer.*

Canon (UK) Ltd. (Photo Dept.), Brent Trading Estate, North Circular Rd., Neasden, London N10 0JF. Tel: 0181 459 1266 *Cameras and accessories.*

Jamie Wood Products Ltd., Cross Street, Polegate, E. Sussex BN26 6BN. Tel: 01323 483813 *Fenman and other hides. Jama IR beam switch.*

Jenoptik (UK) Ltd., PO Box 43, 1 Elstree Way, Borehamwood, Herts. WD6 1NH. Tel: 0181 953 1688 *UK distributor of Sigma cameras and lenses.*

Johnsons Photopia, Hempstalls Lane, Newcastle-under-Lyme, Staffordshire, ST5 0SW. Tel: 01782 753300 *UK importers of Mamiya cameras and Teleplus converters.*

Lakeland Microscopes, Holy Bank, Windermere Road, Lindale, Grange-over-Sands, Cumbria LA11 6LB. Tel: 01539 534737 *Large range of microscopes.*

Lastolite Ltd., 8, Units 1 & 2, Vulkon Court, Hermitage Industrial Estate, Coalville, Leicester LE67 3SW. Tel: 01530 813381 *Portable reflectors and diffusers.*

Minolta (UK) Ltd., Unit 7, Tanners Drive, Blakelands North, Milton Keynes MK14 5BU. Tel: 01908 200400 *Cameras, lenses and accessories.*

Nikon (UK) Ltd., Nikon House, 380 Richmond Road, Kingston-on-Thames, Surrey, KT2 5PR. Tel: 0181 541 4440 *Cameras, lenses and accessories.*

Northern Biological Supplies, 3 Betts Avenue, Martlesham Heath, Ipswich, IP5 7RH. Tel: 01473 623995 *Slides, specimens, instruments and microscopy kits.*

Olympus Optical Co. (UK) Ltd., 2-8 Honduras Street, London EC17 0TX. Tel: 0171 253 2772 *Olympus cameras, lenses and accessories*

Paterson Photographic Ltd., 4 Malthouse Road, Tipton, West Midlands DY4 9EA. Tel: 0121 520 4830 *Benbo tripods and photo accessories.*

Philip Harris Ltd., Novara Group Ltd., Novara House, Excelsior Rd., Asby-de-la-Zouch, Leicester LE65 1NG. Tel: 01530 418000 *Large range of microscopes, both British and foreign, Longworth trap, laboratory equipment.*

RS Components Ltd., PO Box 99, Corby, Northants, NN17 9RS. Tel: 01536 201201 *Electronic components for light-beam switch.*

Tamron (UK) Ltd, 4, Millfield House, Croxley Business Park, Watford, Herts WD1 8YX. Tel: 01923 212214 *Lenses.*

Wildlife Watching Supplies, Town Living Farmhouse, Puddington, Tiverton, Devon EX16 8LW. Tel: 01884 860692 *Camouflage materials, leafscreens, belts, webbing, etc.*

Worldwide Butterflies Ltd., Over Compton, Sherborne, Dorset. Tel: 01935 474608 *British and tropical butterflies and moths.*

USEFUL ORGANISATIONS

The Licensing Section, English Nature, Northminster House, Peterborough, PE1 1UA. Tel: 01733 455000

The Department of the Environment for Northern Ireland Parliament Buildings, Stormont, Belfast, Northern Ireland DT4 3SS. Tel: 01232 63210

The Countryside Council for Wales, Plas Penrhos, Fford Penrhos, Bangor, Gwynedd LL57 2LQ. Tel: 01248 370444

Scottish National Heritage, 12 Hope Terrace, Edinburgh EH9 2AS. Tel: 0131 447 4784

The Royal Society for Nature Conservation, Wildlife Trust Partnership, The Green, Wiltham Park, Waterside South, Lincoln LN5 7JR. Tel: 01522 537424

The Royal Society for the Protection of Birds, The Lodge, Sandy, Bedfordshire, SG19 2DL. Tel: 01767 680551

World Fund for Wildlife (WWF), PO Box 49, Burton-upon-Trent, Staffordshire, DE14 3LQ. Tel 01283 50610

AMERICAN SUPPLIERS AND ORGANISATIONS
EQUIPMENT AND CAMERAS

Bausch & Lomb Incorporated, 635 St Paul Street, Rochester, New York 14602. *Microprojectors, microscopes, other special scientific instruments.*

Carolina Biological Supply Company, 2700 York Road, Burlington, North Carolina and Box 7, Gladstone, Oregon. *Biological models, microscopes, and laboratory equipment.*

General Biological Supply House, Inc. (Turtox), 8200 South Hoyne Avenue, Chicago 20, Illinois.

Canon USA, One Canon Plaza, Lake Success, NY 11042. Tel: 516 488 6700

Mamiya America Corporation, 8 Westchester Plaza, Elmsford, NY 10523. Tel: 914 347 3300

Minolta Corporation, 10 Williams Drive, Ramsey, NJ 07446. Tel: 201 825 4000

Nikon Inc., 1300 Wall Whitman Road, Melville, NY 11747-3064. Tel: 516 547 4200

Olympus Corporation, Crossways Park, Woodbury, NY 11797. Tel: 800 221 3000

Sigma Corporation of America, 15 Fleetwood Court, Ronkonkoma, NY 11779. Tel: 516 585 1144

SPECIALIST EQUIPMENT

Bogen Photo Corporation, 565 East Crescent Ave., Ramsey, NJ 07446. Tel: 201 818 9500 *Bogen/Manfrotto tripods, clamps, stands, Metz flash and accessories.*

Ivan Eberle, PO Box 51307, Pacific Grove, CA 93950-6307. Tel: 408 373 8476 *Light-beam trigger set-ups.*

A. Kenneth Olson, 3 Woodhill Ln., St Paul, MN 55127 2140. Tel: 612 484 0151 *Custom-made, high-voltage, ultra-high-speed flash units and electronic control units.*

Paterson Inc., 4860A Industrial Access Road, Dougsville, GA 30734. *Benbo.*

Protech Inc., 5710-E General Eashington Hwy., Alexandria, VA 22312. Tel: 703 941 9100 Fax: 703 941 8267 *Dale Beam triggers.*

Quantum Instruments, 1075 Stewart Av., Garden City, NY 11530. Tel: 516 222 0611 *Rechargeable battery packs, radio slaves and triggers.*

CONSERVATION ORGANISATIONS

National Wildlife Federation, 1400 16th St. NW, Washington, DC 20036-2266. Tel: 202 797 6800

Nature Conservancy (US), 1815 North Lynn St., Arlington, VA 2209. Tel: 703 841 5300

Wildlife Conservation International, New York Zoological Society, 185th St. and South Blvd., Bronx, NY 10460. Tel: 718 220 5155

World Wildlife Fund (US), 1250 24th St. NW, Washington, DC 20037. Tel: 202 293 4800

ACKNOWLEDGEMENTS

Most of my photographic skills and knowledge have been acquired over many years through reading, experimentation and the constant use of the camera. However I have gained much from studying the work of other nature and wildlife photographers, especially Heather Angel, Stephen Dalton, Laurie Campbell and the American photographer and wordsmith John Shaw; their writing and images are a constant source of pleasure and inspiration.

My sincere thanks to Dr Allan Calder, Dr Mike Kelly and Dr Phoebe Edwards for their interest and encouragement, and to the latter for suggesting several very useful photographic locations.

I am also grateful to Kevin Keatley of Wildlife Watching Supplies (see Appendix) for providing the photographs on pages 8 and 12.

I am greatly indebted to Helen Barker who transformed my much-altered handwritten work into a beautifully presented manuscript, correcting a few errors on the way. My special thanks to Harry Ricketts, Publisher at Fountain Press, who not only afforded me the opportunity to write this book but gave me valuable assistance and guidance throughout its preparation. Grant Bradford, Illustrated Book Design Consultant par excellence, converted the manuscript and a pile of transparencies into an exceptionally attractive, well-balanced book. I thank him most sincerely.

Finally, a very special thank you to my wife Margaret, who encouraged me throughout the project and never complained when my total commitment in time and energy reduced family time to a minimum, while house and garden maintenance had to be postponed yet again.